Failing at Fatherhood

A book for the imperfect father

JACK BARR

Trinity Grace Press

Orlando

Failing at Fatherhood
A book for the imperfect father
by Jack Barr

Trinity Grace Press
www.trinitygracepress.com
email: info@signalmanpublishing.com
Kissimmee, Florida
1-888-907-4423

The foundation of this book is based on real events that have occurred in the author's life as he recalls them. Some names and places have been changed to respect the privacy of others.

ISBN: 978-1-940145-30-3 (sc)
978-1-940145-31-0 (ebook)

Library of Congress Control Number: 2014946441

This book is dedicated to my wife because her patience saved our marriage, to my small group because their endless hours of support prompted my writing, and to my family because they have loved me for the past thirty-five years.

CONTENTS

Foreword

The 21st century American family is in disarray. The ravages of divorce, the harmful effects of abuse and a preoccupation with all things carnal have resulted in a family that is far from the biblical model.

If you add to this scenario, the stress of serving in a foreign mission field and being victimized by sexual abuse as a child, you have an even more difficult situation. Now if you further add a Down syndrome child as your first born, you get a sensing of what Jack Barr was facing. He labels his response to this situation "Failing at Fatherhood," but what he learned about fatherhood can benefit all dads.

The Bible sets a high standard for dads, a standard most of us are not even close to achieving. I had it easy growing up. I was raised by Godly parents in an uncomplicated rural environment. My childhood was, by comparison to Jack's, idyllic. The temptations to do drugs, drink or be promiscuous were much less than they are today.

But I also had a great role model as a dad. "Chap" was an industrious, hard-working man who came to Christ as an adult and devoted himself to being a Godly man and father. He lived under the umbrella of Deuteronomy 6:1-7 to "Love the LORD your God with all your heart and with all your soul and with all your strength." My parents impressed on me this ideal and I grew up fearing the LORD and keeping His commands to the extent a normal kid could in the 1950s. But I didn't have to figure out how to be a father, I merely followed the loving model my dad gave to me.

We are called to be Godly fathers today and I think this calling is more important than ever as we observe a culture out of control, one that has abandoned, for the most part, biblical instruction and values. That's where Jack's book is so helpful. He doesn't sugarcoat it; he is brutally honest and self-critical.

Our commitment to be Godly men and fathers is more important than ever, and I wonder if there's any hope of our survival as a culture unless our dads rise to the occasion. Osten Sorenson said: "A child is not likely to find a father in God unless he finds something of God in his father." This is no easy task as Jack explains, and it is a challenge more and more men are neglecting in the pursuit of pleasure, success, or worldly rewards.

Jack confesses that he is deeply ashamed of his initial reaction to the birth of his Down syndrome daughter, Marley, but that is why he is sharing his story. In the book, he describes himself as "just a regular guy trying to figure out how to be a father and provide everything I can for my daughter that has Down syndrome." The book itself is anything but regular or ordinary. It is honest and helpful. It provides insight into how all us dads can accomplish our vital job in a God-honoring way.

Failing at Fatherhood is artfully and candidly written to evoke painful, but therapeutic memories of when we, as fathers, may have fallen short of the high standard set by our Heavenly Father. It reminds us of the important calling we have as dads, especially in the 21st century when fathers are less and less a part of the family and contribute less and less to helping our kids grow to be responsible, mature, Christian adults.

The subtitle Jack added to his book, "A book for the imperfect father," describes us all to one extent or the other and sets the stage for what you will encounter in the following pages. Jack provides solid scriptural support for his thesis and applies the Bible well. Each chapter also contains a helpful assignment, that may assist you in uncovering or resolving any dysfunctional past relationships with your Heavenly Father, with your earthly father, living or deceased, or, most importantly with your own kids.

I thank God that Jack has written an honest and helpful book that will benefit other parents with similar challenges. But beyond that, everyone who is challenged in life will benefit by this story and Jack's experience.

Bob Russell
Retired Senior Minister
Southeast Christian Church
http://www.bobrussell.org/

Prologue

April 14, 2011

Consider it pure joy, my brothers and sisters, whenever you face trials of many kinds. (James 1:2 NIV)

I hear her breathing—that raspy up and down cadence I have listened to for the past three weeks. The relentless noise makes it impossible to sleep. It is 2:00am and I have been listening to this creature agonize me for the past two hours. Why do I fear her so much? She is my own flesh and blood, yet I lie here silently wondering if I will be here in the morning. What kind of father am I? What kind of father secretly plots opportunities to quietly disappear in the middle of the night instead of facing another day with his daughter?

For two weeks I prayed for God to heal her, but, of course, he ignored my desperate cries. What kind of God would allow my daughter to suffer when I offered my own life to heal her? God and I both know the future she will have if she continues to live. She will be mocked, pitied, ignored, and told how she is different from everyone else. When people look at her, they will only notice her differences and not her similarities. The Down syndrome parents I read about are only tricking themselves into thinking their child is normal. All of my friends have normal children whom they can watch grow and develop, but not us. My daughter will never go to college, never get married, never have children, and never experience the intimacy of being touched by someone who truly loves her.

Is this your idea of fairness, God? Supposedly you are just, but after serving you for seven years in Thailand, you have punished my daughter and my family. Instead of blessing me with a normal child, I lay here listening to this human you created and know she will never succeed in this world. No matter what she does, she will always be seen as the little girl with Down syndrome.

Her breathing is louder now. God, why am I here? Why is Marley the daughter you chose to put in my life? I have already failed her, my wife, and myself. Just twelve months ago my life was completely different. Now I hate this extra chromosome I can't see, I hate my wife for helping me create this child, I hate you for not answering my prayers, and I hate myself for having to live with this unchangeable situation until the day I die. Instead of Marley not waking up in the morning, how about you let me die tonight?

I can still hear her raspy up-and-down breathing. I am a worthless excuse for a father, and I truly believe my wife would be better off without me. Truthfully I am disgusted by the pathetic title I now carry as a dad. What kind of father becomes fearful of his own child because of two words—Down syndrome—said by a doctor?

Introduction: Let's Put the Cards on the Table

He replied, "Because you have so little faith. Truly I tell you, if you have faith as small as a mustard seed, you can say to this mountain, 'Move from here to there,' and it will move. Nothing will be impossible for you." (Matthew 17:20 NIV)

You might have already developed a strong opinion about me based on the opening of this book. Most people I meet usually have very distinct reactions to my story. These reactions are based on my willingness to share the deep innermost parts of my soul. As you read along, you need to understand that I am going to share and discuss issues which will make you uncomfortable. However, these issues are the ones that I was taught to suppress and never share with another person because I was a man. Talking and sharing was for the other gender, so I bottled up all of my emotions and was expected to "deal" with it. So, as we begin this journey, be prepared for an openness that is difficult, but necessary for our roles as successful fathers. This willingness to be open is not only going to be the roadmap of my story, but also a challenge for you in your life as a father.

The first reaction I usually encounter when sharing my story is sympathy for my situation. These sympathizers are usually parents that have encountered the inner turmoil I described in the previous pages. They have had those dark moments in the middle of the night contemplating the worst of thoughts. They have been crushed by the overwhelming power of depression and have emerged from that disgusting tunnel of hopelessness. They understand the pain when instantly their child is not the child they had imagined.

Parents of "normal children" often tell me that all children fail our expectations throughout life and parents with special needs children are no exception. But parents of special needs children understand that the difference lies in the empathetic voice of the doctor when he or she tells you that your newborn baby has a disability. The doctor calmly explains how it will take longer for your child to achieve certain milestones in life and he or she may never be independent. All the dreams you had for your child—professional athlete, actor, minister, college graduate, doctor, president, wife, father, scientist, astronaut, musician—have to be adjusted to a "realistic expectation" in a matter of seconds because your child is "special."

The next group I usually encounter is probably the hardest group for me to interact with because I believe they are partially correct in their opinion of me. They think I am a worthless father and I only care about myself. When I first shared my story with

CNN, I read through many of the comments and there was one that still haunts me most nights:

> Well congratulations to this man, he did what he was suppose to do and stayed with his family. Big deal—he loves his daughter that he created. Why do we praise a man for being a worthless father? There will be a day in the future that he will regret sharing this story and his daughter will hate him. This guy cares about nothing except himself and his own desires in life. This guy is pathetic and his family would be better off without him because he will probably leave them one day in the future, anyway. (http://edition.cnn.com/2013/06/27/health/down-syndrome-father-essay/)

When I first wrote my story, I never thought people would have extremely different reactions. It surprised me when I started reading the negative comments and encountered the overall bitterness of some people. Unfortunately, I mostly agree with the writer's comment above. I am deeply ashamed of my initial reaction to my own daughter, but that is why I am sharing my story. I was a selfish father who was only thinking about how my child's condition would change my life. I was already placing my "missed opportunities" on my daughter even before her first breath. I know every day there are fathers like me who experience the joy of having a new child along with the agony of a devastating diagnosis. They are faced with a decision and must choose to stay or leave a child who is viewed differently by this world. I want to share that I doubted, I contemplated the worst, I was angry at my wife, and I hated God, but now, two years later, I embrace leaving work at 5:00pm so I can go home to kiss, hug, and play with my beautiful daughter every night.

The last group of people I have encountered the past few years are confused Christians. They approach me with a justified anger in their eyes and ask, "How can you doubt God's will for your life?" Usually, my answer to that is, "I don't know." I majored in theological studies, I was ordained in the Christian church, and I currently live in Thailand teaching at an international Christian school. My current life is based on serving God overseas to reach people who have never experienced the love of Christ. Yet, when that doctor looked me in the eyes and said, "I think your child has mongoloid features," my entire faith collapsed. I felt like I had followed God's calling for my life, but here I was having a daughter that would be different from everyone I knew. My initial thoughts were, "This is not fair," and, "I blame you, God."

Fellow Christians preached to me about an unshakable faith, but I have never experienced that in my life. Either my faith is a lackluster excuse for a relationship with God, or God *does* expect us as believers to question the events that are happening around us. In response to my fellow believers who are disappointed in my faithless doubt, all I can say is that questioning God led me to talking with God. For the past two years I have *really* talked to God. I talk to God in the same manner I would talk to my wife sitting at the dinner table. I openly share with him my anger and disappointment about my child's disability. Sometimes this will last for hours and involve screaming, fighting, crying, and praying but I know this has helped me build a stronger relationship with my Creator. My faith is still not without doubt, but now I believe in a God who I can actually share my life with and can handle my real, unsuppressed emotions.

There is nothing special about me. I grew up in a small town in the South, went to a small college, became a Christian, and decided to serve God overseas through teaching. I am just a regular guy trying to figure out how to be a father and provide everything I can for my daughter who has Down syndrome. This is my story of fear, failure, faith, acceptance, and reconciliation. I conclude this book by writing a letter to my daughter about this experience and my failures as her father. Feel free to cry, scream, and laugh as I share with you my journey into fatherhood. Regardless of how you feel about my story or me, I think it is one that needs to be heard.

Today

Fathers must figure out how to survive today before focusing on yesterday or tomorrow.

Chapter 1

Welcome Marley

I prayed for this child, and the Lord has granted me what I asked of him. So now I give him to the Lord. For his whole life he will be given over to the Lord. (1 Samuel 1:27-28 NIV)

March 20, 2011—right now I am sitting here, wondering what the remainder of my life will entail. My life has been completely transformed in the past twenty-four hours, and I have experienced things that every husband should be prepared to face with his wife. My wife told me I should prepare by reading the books she had bought, but who wants to read books written by doctors? We have been married for nine years and have faced many difficult situations together, so I knew I would be prepared for this next step in our life. Unfortunately, as I sit here the day after our daughter's birth, I am still overcome with fear, concern, and anxiety. Every ten minutes I walk down to the nursery to see if our daughter is still breathing or not. I watch my wife try to recover from labor by eating broth for her main meal. I am also still in shock at how inadequately I performed as a husband in my wife's greatest time of need.

The miracle of birth and the heart-wrenching fear of labor were unlike anything I have experienced in my life. Watching the misery of my wife trying to dislodge this creature from her womb was a horrific event for me. "Helplessness" is the only word I can think to describe my uselessness yesterday. While I watched my beautiful wife who I had brought to the other side of the world grimace in pain, the only thought circulating in my mind was, "She is going to die." No husband wants to phone his in-laws from across the world and explain that their daughter had died while trying to give birth to their first grandchild. For eighteen hours my wife suffered through labor with no assistance from painkillers, the medical staff, or me. The doctor visited us every few hours in the natural birth room saying that everything looked good and for us to just hang in there.

*Listen you *** of a *****, things are not fine! My wife is in incredible pain and you think everything is fine? How about you do your job and help my wife get this creature out of her? She is throwing up, sprawled out motionless on the floor and pleading for help, and all you can offer is 'hang in there?'*

Of course, none of this was said because a good Christian man should not speak with this tone, but distressing moments can lead to some bitter thoughts. Watching your spouse suffer with no possible remedy can drive a man to madness. This leads to desperate feelings of failure as a caretaker. How inadequate I felt while watching my wife suffer from unbelievable pain and neither the doctor nor I could do anything to relieve her agony.

Suddenly the contractions were disrupting Marley's heart rate. This caused immediate distress and concern in the medical staff at the hospital. Marley's heartbeat would hover around one hundred and forty beats a minute, but when Jana would have a contraction, Marley's heart rate would drop below seventy. The doctor told us to prepare for an immediate C-section and the nurse wheeled Jana away to an operating room. Another nurse led me to a changing room where I was dressed up with scrubs and a hat. My wife was suddenly taken away from me and there I sat in a room wearing a ridiculous costume. After about twenty minutes, the nurse came for me. She walked me into a room that reminded me of those horror films where people become dismembered.

Jana was lying on the table with a sheet separating her head from the remainder of her body. The nurse directed me to a chair beside Jana's head so I could talk to her during the process. Jana looked up at me and I could see the fear of life in her beautiful blue eyes. Immediately, I heard my father's voice echoing in my mind: "Time to be a man. Your wife needs you and this is the time to forget about your own ridiculous fears and support your life companion. If you can't be a man now for your wife then you will never amount to anything in this world." Instantly, I took a deep breath and said, "Well, this looks like fun." She smiled at me and said, "We'll see."

As the process began, I could tell the sedative was starting to take away Jana's sense of awareness. Every few seconds she would ask me if we were almost finished. I kept assuring her that the doctors were almost finished as I gently held her hand. The entire event took about thirty minutes and I said very little to her during the C-section operation. Comforting her did not involve many words, but instead a willingness to hold her hand and reassure her that everything was ok. Oftentimes in life, we say too much when comforting others instead of listening, and this was a time Jana desired a companion and not a lecture. She didn't need me to fix things with my words, but instead she needed me to be present experiencing the journey with her. Being beside her and holding her hand was the commitment she needed to feel safe and secure. Nine years earlier as we pledged our vows for life during an outdoor autumn wedding, I was simply thinking about the upcoming honeymoon night. But I am sure Jana was envisioning moments like this in which I would be there holding her hand as our first child entered the world. Funny how often men and women vary in thought process! Missing that moment for my wife would have been unacceptable in my role as a husband. Of course, you cannot always be there when the love of your life needs you, but when you can, make sure you are. Nothing should hinder our role as being fearless protectors when our wives are in their greatest times of despair.

The Carnage

Do you ever pass a car crash and know that it's best not to look, but you somehow cannot help your natural inclination to see the carnage? Well, I looked over the curtain about halfway through the C-section procedure to see what was happening "down there" with the doctors. "Great Scott!"—to quote our fabulous character Doctor Emmett Brown—were the only words I could summon to describe what I saw on that operating table. Certainly there are things we should never see unless we are medical doctors. The destruction of flesh I watched transpire over the head divider would make the strongest men flinch. It reminded me of a toddler eating pasta with spaghetti sauce. The entire lower part of Jana's body had been turned over to two children with forks pulling and pushing through her organs like they were eating their first bowl of spaghetti. Even now when I watch monster Marley tear through some scrumptious pasta, I have to suppress images of the doctors that night cutting into Jana's womb to retrieve our first child. While blood and organs were thrown around like ziti shells, the nauseating sound of suction happened every few seconds while a nurse "cleared out" an area so the doctors could see. The climatic moment that brought me back to reality was when the two doctors pulled on Jana's abdominal cage with all of their might. I quickly realized that it was time for me to return to my spot of comforting Jana on the other side of the curtain. The picture of watching two doctors play tug of war with Jana's internal organs was enough medical interning for me. Holding Jana's hand and reassuring her that everything was going to be ok seemed like a great job at the moment compared to the other side of that curtain. But then I heard a cry.

Joining the Club

Seeing your child for the first time is the purest form of love that you can ever experience as a father. Watching our baby emerge from my wife's womb was astonishing. We were taught about it in school, watched simulations of it on TV, and read about it in books, but when that moment of life materializes in front of your own eyes, describing the event is virtually impossible. Marley was just a figment of my imagination until the moment she left Jana's womb and embraced the world. Of course, I felt her kick in Jana's womb and watched the misery of pregnancy for the past nine months, but for me, the reality of Marley's existence did not happen until I heard that fierce cry from the other side of the curtain. The love I thought could never be duplicated for another person besides my wife actually magnified ten times at the precise moment my new daughter arrived. I literally felt like the Grinch at Christmas when his heart grew after embracing the spirit of Christmas. Unfortunately, the concern I had for Jana during the entire procedure was stripped immediately from my mind because of the abundant joy I felt by being part of the new life I helped create. Fathering a child and watching her enter this world is one of the few moments that can never be corrupted by anything or anyone. Observing Marley take her first breath will forever be one of the single greatest moments of my life.

Once they pulled Marley out, they began performing numerous tests on her. If I had read the books that Jana left by my bedside every night, then I would have known this is a common practice know as the Apgar test. Watching them pull and push on Marley aroused a protective fury in me, and I stood up to confront the situation. The doctor, knowing I had lost all rational judgment, told me she looked great and had passed the Apgar tests. Dumbfounded I muttered "ok" and continued to stare at him with no clear direction on my next move. The doctor, sensing I had lost all rational judgment, told me they needed to take Jana to the recovery room for a few hours and that I should go down to the nursery to see my daughter. "Jana. That's right—Jana is still here and needs me to comfort her. How could I forget about her so quickly?" Even though Jana was still partially sedated, she looked at me, smiled and said, "Go. " I kissed her and proceeded to stumble down the hallway in search of the nursery.

Held Her Hand

I stood outside the nursery peering in the window, contemplating two things before opening the door: how was I going to find my daughter; and how was I going to talk to the nurses when they could not speak English? For the past eight years, I would just abandon the situation when I could not communicate and move on without the item or answer to my question. I began to smile at the thought of sitting in the waiting room for hours not seeing my daughter because I was too scared to go in and try to communicate with the nurses. Jana would certainly have had some choice words for me if our daughter spent her first few hours alone because her father was too cowardly to cross a language barrier.

I could not resist any longer and no one was coming to help me even though I was staring in the nursery like a child at the zoo. So I swallowed my fear, swung open the door, charged past the changing area, and started walking around the various cribs looking for the little white baby. All at once nurses appeared from every corner of the room and began yelling at me while frantically swinging their arms. An older nurse grabbed me by the arm and sternly led me towards the door I had just entered.

As she pushed me out the door, I quickly became angry and started walking back towards her—I wanted to see my daughter. She raised her hand and gave me the universal stop motion. I stopped and looked her straight in the eyes. She smiled and pointed toward the main thing I had missed before barging in the room. There, beside the door, was a little sign that said in English, "Please change shoes and clothes before entering the nursery." I lowered my head in shame and went back to change my clothes. After I had finished, she asked me in broken English for the name of my child. I wanted to scream, "Probably the only white kid in the entire nursery right now," but instead I just said, "Marley Barr." Once again she smiled and led me to a crib in the corner of the room.

Overwhelming emotions took control of my body while looking into that crib of pale skin and blonde hair. I started to cry so the nurse put her hand on my shoulder. Marley was so beautiful. The little creature was the most beautiful thing I had ever witnessed in my life and by the grace of God, I was a part of her life. The nurse brought over a stool and I positioned myself beside her. In a few minutes the nurse left us alone, and without asking permission from the germ police, I reached in the crib and held her hand.

Talking to Marley

For two hours I sat beside my daughter's crib when she was first born. While Jana was in the recovery room sleeping, I was in the nursery staring amazed at the being laying in front of me. Marley mostly slept during that time but the awe of the moment kept me by her side looking at her. I could not comprehend that only twenty-four hours earlier, she was just a possibility—now she was a reality entrusted to me for the remainder of my life. As my mind tried to steal the moment with thoughts of responsibility and fear, I suppressed those thoughts and truly enjoyed the moment of life.

There are very few times in life that I "remain still" and absorb the richness of the moment, but on that night I did. Sitting in that nursery with my daughter is an experience that I will never forget, one that can never be altered by the evil of this world. For two hours, my daughter was a perfect little creature completely made in the image of God.

As we bonded in that nursery, I began telling Marley stories about her family and living in Thailand. Obviously she could not understand me, but there was an enormous amount of information I had to pass on to her during those moments. I talked to her about Jana, my father, our family in the States, our family in Thailand, and mostly about how much I already loved her. She slept peacefully after the traumatic experience of birth, but I continued talking non-stop about life before her arrival, and what I envisioned life being now that she had made a grand entry into this world. As admiration for my daughter quickly grew in those first few hours in the nursery, little did I know that the birth of my daughter would not be the most significant life-changing moment that weekend, but instead the news we would receive three days later as we prepared to finally go home as a family.

Relive the Moment of Birth

The overwhelming sense of joy you felt as that first child was being born needs to be shared with him or her. I have one child so I am not sure how the feelings duplicate with multiple children, but I can tell you that when Marley arrived in the world I felt something exhilarating. Sit down with your child and tell him or her about that marvelous moment. You don't have to be graphic but share the joy you felt. Tell him or her about the time leading up to the birth, the rush to the hospital, the chaos of labor, and the overwhelming love you felt as he or she was born. Maybe you were not there. If you were not, then I would encourage you to sit down with someone that was there and have that person tell the story to you and your child. Sharing about your child's birth is an exciting thing and will strengthen that bond we sometimes are not able to experience as fathers of newborns.

Chapter 2

Embracing Down Syndrome

I am worn out from my groaning. All night long I flood my bed with weeping and drench my couch with tears. My eyes grow weak with sorrow; they fail because of all my foes. Away from me, all you who do evil, for the Lord has heard my weeping. The Lord has heard my cry for mercy; the Lord accepts my prayer.
(Psalm 6:6-9 NIV)

We spent three days in the hospital while Jana was recovering and we were learning to be parents. There were some early signs that should have been a warning to us, but we were rookies in the vocation of parenthood. Marley had a tough time breastfeeding at first. We were not sure what the problem was and the nurse did not offer much advice, but Marley was having a difficult time latching. Looking back on it now, not knowing the underlying problem was probably extremely beneficial for Marley, because my wife was determined that Marley would breastfeed. If they had told us that low muscle tone was common in babies with Down syndrome, then we might have made an exception and given her a bottle. Instead, Jana worked with her for hours and finally got her to drink some milk through breastfeeding.

Another red flag was Marley's love for sleep and lack of crying. She cried when she was first born, but cried very little after her birth. She slept for numerous hours without waking regardless of hunger pains. Later in life, it seemed the only thing ingrained in her little mind was eating, but during those first three days we would have to wake her from a deep sleep in order to feed her.

Even though these issues were present when Marley was born, there were no major indications that maybe something was not quite right. We were overwhelmed with excitement and were trying to learn how to care for this little newborn, so we dismissed these nuisances as being part of her personality. The hours before we left the hospital, we found out that these "personality traits" indicated more than what we had initially thought.

During Jana's pregnancy, we did the usual tests and ultrasounds at the hospital. After the main ultrasound in which they measured numerous parts and took various readings, they gave us an approximation of the chances of Marley having Down syndrome. The report, which we still have today, told us that she had a one in 18,000 chance of having Down syndrome.

That dreadful morning, Jana was taking a shower and I was packing up in preparation for our trip home. I had spent the morning getting the car seat perfect and wondering how slow I would need to drive in Bangkok traffic to preserve the life of my daughter. At that moment the infant pediatrician came in and said she wanted to talk to me. I told her that Jana was showering and suggested she come back in a bit, but she wanted to talk to me alone. I thought, "Ok, this probably has something to do with insurance." She looked me directly in the eyes and said, "I think Marley has Down syndrome features."

My thoughts stopped. Car seats, crazy traffic, and everything else that had dominated my morning dissipated into oblivion. Closing my eyes and holding back tears, I said, "Down syndrome?" Immediately I screamed for Jana as if the doctor had just told me that Marley had died. Jana came crashing out of the shower in nothing but a towel and shrieked, "What is wrong?" I yelled, "The doctor said Marley has Down syndrome."

At that moment I left this world and began heading to another place between life and death. Grabbing my chest, I fell to the couch and Jana wailed. Jana pushed the emergency button in the room as I crumpled to the floor. I could not breathe. Suddenly I became nauseous and felt my body entering a paralyzed state. It was too overwhelming to stop so I closed my eyes and drifted away to a peaceful place until the shaking of a Thai doctor brought me back to reality on the emergency room operating table.

The first question I asked was, "Where is Jana?" He told me to relax and began explaining what a panic attack was in simple terms. He then informed me that the sedative they had given me had enabled my body to calm down so they could check my vitals. He told me that everything was fine, but next time I should breathe deeply when I felt the onset of a panic attack. *Thanks for the advice, Doc.* Readers, if the doctor tells you that your first-born child has Down syndrome, you should breathe deeply and everything will be ok.

Once he finished his lecture, I asked if I could go back to my wife's room. He said yes, and the head nurse led me back to the maternity ward where Jana was waiting for me. As I walked in the room, I saw Jana, the baby doctor from hell, and the obstetrician that had delivered Marley. The OB walked up and gave me a hug. He looked me in the eyes and said, "I don't see it." Two doctors from the same hospital disagreed on the subject of my daughter having Down syndrome—was this some cruel joke? For the next hour, the two doctors talked to us about the different indicators they saw which both suggested and did not suggest Down syndrome.

Sitting in that room as new parents and listening to doctors try to explain that our daughter *might* have Down syndrome was one of the worst experiences in my life. *This is my daughter, not some experimental riddle that we are trying to solve. Just give us an answer! Is that too much to ask on the day we are going home as a family for the first time?* Finally, the evil baby doctor said they would draw blood and let us know in three weeks if Marley had Down syndrome or not—*three weeks!* I asked why we needed to wait three weeks, and she stated that the test took two weeks in Thailand and she would be out of town the third week, so it had to be after that. *Thanks, Doc, we would hate to inconvenience you with our small dilemma. We will just spend the next three weeks wondering if our daughter has little ole Down syndrome or not. No big deal.*

Entering the Pit of Darkness

Growing up in my family was not a good place to accept the idea of suffering from depression. An extended family member once had a bout with depression and it was not a good reflection on our family because she was viewed as weak. When you grow up in the Deep South, things like suffering from depression are often viewed as a lack of faith. Many families believe you are having a mental breakdown because you don't really believe in God or because you are too fragile to handle your own life. Unfortunately, I fell into this way of thinking when discussing my family member with my cousins at a family reunion. In the famous words of my dad, I told my cousin that this person should just "suck it up" and stop crying about everything. How easy it is to judge when you are a tough young boy. Little did I know that she was struggling with spousal issues and had even contemplated leaving as an escape from the torment of her husband.

The pit of depression is a lonely place, and I have grasped that few people are willing or able to help you find hope in the darkness. When the doctor uttered the words, "Down syndrome" on that day, I plunged head first into a lake of pain that took me an entire year to emerge from. Even my own wife became extremely frustrated with my condition because of my lack of usefulness in helping with Marley that first year.

Battling depression is like any other obstacle in life, and if you have not experienced it, then helping someone who is depressed is virtually impossible. The inner abyss of depression led me to appalling thoughts about my own life, daughter, wife, and God. The demons caressed my depression into a despair that I believed would engulf my life forever, and the only escape I could imagine was ending the torment permanently.

It began as a shock. The doctor must be lying—how could my daughter be born with Down syndrome? My wife was a high level gymnast, I had played collegiate baseball, and we had both passionately followed God to work in Thailand. This couldn't be true. Our genes and commitment to God could not be thwarted by some Thai doctor who wasn't even sure if our daughter had Down syndrome. We were "normal" parents, living a regular life, so how could something "unusual" not only happen to us, but also be a staple of our family until the day we died? From this moment forward, we would be labeled as the "the parents of a special needs child" and escaping that society stamp would not be possible for the remainder of our lives. That was the phrase that began to overcome my thoughts, desires, and nightmares: "the remainder of my life."

Death is different. The death of a loved one is a permanent event that cannot be altered or changed. When you bury that significant person in your life, you know the event is final and nothing can bring that person back into your life. When my father died, I entered into a deep sadness that was suppressed with drugs, alcohol, and sex. For over a year I lived a numb life that had little meaning or purpose. The escape I required was occupying my mind and body with things that would distract me from the death of my father. I was able to avoid embracing the loss of my father by filling my life with abusive substances. Once I emerged from this drunken state a year later, I began meeting with a counselor who helped me deal with the emotions of losing my father. After my father's death, I found a way to escape the pain of losing him because of the finality of death.

Marley's birth was not like my father's death. There was no escape in sight. Every time I came home, she was there. Every time I got up, she was there. Everyone I met asked me how she was doing, so I was unable to use the same suppression mechanism that I had previously used when dealing with my father's sickness and death. It is very difficult for a man, working at a Christian school in the middle of Asia, to forgo everything and enter into a world of drugs and alcohol like he did in college. Substances could not help me with this journey because I had to keep my job to support my family, and I was entrenched in a Christian community that had to know everything about my life and spiritual welfare. Knowing that my co-workers were aware of the circumstances surrounding Marley's birth was a living hell for me at the time, but looking back on it now, I realize the staff at my school helped me stay accountable during that desperate year.

I had been working in Bangkok at an international Christian school for the past eight years. Working there during Marley's birth was both a blessing and a headache for me. At the time, I hated that people would routinely check up on me throughout the day. Co-workers would just drop by my office or class to express their concern. I became that *unstable teacher who needed guidance*. However, without the intervention of the school community, I would have embraced those dangerous old habits that I had turned to after the death of my father. Those old habits would do nothing to help me confront the pain of my child being different, but instead, I realized, they would only numb my feelings of existence. Thankfully, the support I received refused to let me do anything other than confront this traumatic experience head on. When my father died, I said goodbye to him for the remainder of my life. When Marley was born, however, the realization that the rest of my life would be spent raising a daughter with Down syndrome crushed my soul.

Anger is the only word I can find to describe the first two weeks of life with Marley in our apartment. The bitterness I felt was split between three people and I had to encounter them every day of my life.

When I wrote the CNN article several months before this book, a commenter stated, “I would have left my wife for giving me a disabled child.” Unfortunately, that is how I felt when Marley first arrived. The only thing that dominated my thoughts was anger toward my wife, Marley, and God. Even though we had to wait several weeks for the official diagnosis, I began convincing myself that Marley had Down syndrome because I thought it would be easier when we got the test results. My wife refused to accept anything without official proof, which quickly increased the separation in our marriage. Jana was still holding out hope while I was already distancing myself from her.

This self-defeating acceptance led me to become very resentful towards my wife. Talking to Jana and interacting with her became a spiteful exchange in which I wanted to humiliate her as much as humanly possible. She was the partner that had led me to this life of misery, and I thought she should be punished for it. The doctors told us that having a child with Down syndrome was a genetic abnormality, but I knew it was Jana who had passed down the genetic difference. At night, I laid in bed staring at my sleeping wife; a depth of maddening anger, which leads people to committing horrific acts, magnified as I thought about our inability to have a “normal” child.

During those moments, regrettably, the only strain of self-control that would keep me from lashing out at her was the vivid image of me spending the remainder of my life in prison. During those terrible nights, I was unable to see the magnificent woman who had led me to a deeper relationship with God, but rather I simply saw a woman who threatened my comfortable life. Evil desires would enter my mind and echo that I must do something to change this shameful situation before it ruined *my* life. My new life that first year consisted of me plotting ways to leave Jana and never embrace the day I heard my daughter say "daddy."

Jana, on the other hand, immediately bonded with Marley. She was spending an enormous amount of time feeding and caring for her, but I was stuck heading back to work. This deepened even further my depressed state because I viewed myself as an outcast from my own family.

Sometimes at night while rocking Marley to sleep, I would question why I felt extremely disconnected from her. This led me to develop feelings of separation and a lack of empathy towards Marley. Instead of embracing her for the beautiful person she was, my mind was flooded with fear and anger about who she would become as she grew older. For that first year, I never savored the joys of being a father while rocking my daughter. Instead I would only focus on the negative aspects of my perceived future with her while ignoring the charming joy of cradling my own child. During the beginning of Marley's life, I felt robbed of a happiness that most fathers experience and this led me to blame Marley. In reality, my own selfish desires and faults were to blame, but I believed the lack of connection with my daughter was because of her condition. How ignorant a father can be when he is only focused on himself!

Jana and Marley were bonding more and more every day, yet I was becoming more distant. After a few months, I became an absent father who was uninterested in holding or interacting with his own daughter. Feeling unable to bond with Marley, I abandoned her and plunged head-first into my work and anything that kept me away from home. I took every opportunity I could find to be away from Jana and Marley so I would not feel the shame that accompanied my failures as a father. Marley became an object of my anger, not just because she had Down syndrome, but also because every day I witnessed the blooming bond between her and Jana that was absent of me. I was unable to overcome my own selfish motives and this led to a nonexistent relationship with my daughter for the first year of her life.

Besides my wife and daughter, God also received a great deal of my fury. Our school has a weight room that is connected to a gymnasium on our campus. Late at night, I would leave my apartment and go to the weight room to be alone with God. For hours I would punch a heavy bag until my hands were raw and bleeding out of the rage I felt for being cursed. This continued for many months and only one person would be pictured on that heavy bag while I desperately punched it in anger—God. I used this time to lash out at God for punishing my daughter. The aloneness of that weight room and gym at night gave me an outlet to scream, fight, and curse at God with no one else present. This was impossible to do during the day because I had to carry on the persona of a Christian dealing with my depression in a civilized way. How can a Christian audibly curse God and display his displeasure with him in front of other believers? That bag became the focal point of all of my madness, and I even often challenged

God to meet me in that dirty weight room most nights.

Pushing my body till exhaustion not only benefited me physically, but it also opened an avenue for me to share my inner demons with God. God was the one to blame for this life I had inherited, and I was not going to stand by and let him "get away with it." For my entire life, I had feared the idea of an eternity of torment, but honestly, some nights I would sit exhausted in that dark weight room and welcome thoughts of being separated from God for an eternity. On those malicious evenings, I was teetering on the brink of embracing a life of evil.

In the scriptures, we see examples of people being "demon possessed." I had always scoffed at the notion of someone being demon possessed because I did not really understand that concept until I experienced those repulsive nights of confronting God. In those murky evenings, I would envision a life of rebellion against God and doing everything possible to hurt God, my family, and my friends. Harmful thoughts would creep into my mind. The only comfort I found was in imagining ways to punish others or myself. That thin line of insanity was crossed only in my thoughts during those occasions, but it gave me a glimpse of the evil creature I could become if those maddening thoughts overtook my life.

Do I believe it was demon possession? I don't know, but I learned for the first time how horrible I could become if I did not get my thoughts and my life under control. Being angry with Jana and Marley was difficult enough to overcome, but it did not compare with the resentment I felt towards God. God was at the center of the storm, and Marley, Jana, and my past had to be reconciled before approaching the chasm between my Creator and me.

Honesty with God is hard for some Christians to embrace. We are taught from an early age not to question God or his will for our lives. We are guided by examples in the Bible in which we rejoice in the suffering we receive in this life because of the rewards we will receive in eternity. The problem for me is I welcome peace in my life. When a problem occurs either within my life or my family's, I want to find a resolution. That is impossible to do when you cannot directly attack the problem head on. When Jana and I have a fight, it usually takes someone saying, "I am sorry," a little bit of laughing about the argument, and some love making to reach a place of reconciliation. When arguments manifest, I search for a course of action that will lead to a solution. This approach did not work with Marley because the source of my anger—God—was not physically present. There was nothing I could do in that moment to change Marley or this new life before me. Hating God gave me the outlet I needed to blame someone for the problem. Fixing the problem depended on me talking openly with God.

There is a story in the Scriptures that describes a man named Jacob wrestling with God. There are numerous explanations concerning this story and you can lodge some significant theological debates on the passage, but that is not my purpose here. I reference this story because we must be willing to embrace conflict with God. Genesis 32:28 (NLT) states, "From now on you will be called Israel, because you have fought with God and with men and have won." (Jacob's name was changed to Israel)

A few years ago, some people criticized some of the writings of Mother Teresa when she openly shared her struggles with God while ministering to the poor. But Mother Teresa understood that these struggles are necessary in our relationship with God. I believe God wants honest followers. Unfortunately we have been taught to question nothing, but how is that humanly possible? What we often do is stay silent, not question anything, and hide our raw emotions. This is not healthy spiritually or physically. Did I cross some lines the nights I openly challenged God? Of course I did, but those moments freed my soul because I was baring everything to my Creator. When you hurt, God hurts, so why would God not want us to share the inner turmoil of our soul? We need to encourage one another to wrestle with God. We will not win the battle, but at least we have the opportunity to fight. This struggle enables us to learn lessons that could never be taught without engaging God.

Embrace the Fury

We all will have times when our world is turned upside down and we will enter into an intense state of rage. The problem we have as fathers is that often we have no outlet for our fury. It will attack us when we least expect it, and we have to find a suppressing mechanism to keep from physically hurting someone at that exact moment. From my experience, I have learned this is not beneficial for the problem or for us. When that anger comes, we need to find an outlet or it will eventually build into an incurable bitterness.

Find your angry place (like finding your happy place), a place you can be alone and unleash every ounce of rage you have in a safe setting. For me, that was the weight room at our school in the evenings. I would lift, punch a heavy bag, and break chairs against the wall when needed. We all need that place of solitude where we can unleash that caveman aggression that overcomes us when we become angry. I would push myself to complete exhaustion and it would help me deal with that uncontrollable rage I felt at the time. While pushing myself physically, I would also engage God spiritually. Confronting God openly about my hatred and my situation forced me to bare my soul. Punching that heavy bag would have had little significance in my situation if I were not also wrestling with God. You need to find times and places to let yourself go and encounter God. These encounters can help you overcome the harsh realities of life and teach you that God is there during the difficult times.

Chapter 3

Looking for an Escape Hatch

Then the Lord God provided a leafy plant and made it grow up over Jonah to give shade for his head to ease his discomfort, and Jonah was very happy about the plant. But at dawn the next day God provided a worm, which chewed the plant so that it withered. When the sun rose, God provided a scorching east wind, and the sun blazed on Jonah's head so that he grew faint. He wanted to die, and said, "It would be better for me to die than to live." But God said to Jonah, "Is it right for you to be angry about the plant?" "It is," he said. "And I'm so angry I wish I were dead."
(Jonah 4:6-9 NIV)

I had to reach out. My life was slowly crumbling around me and my family was on the brink of separation. Every time I thought about Marley's future and the pain she would experience, I immediately thought about my own escape. How could I escape when things got dreadful? The first thought to enter my mind when this fear would overcome me was suicide. It was not that I wanted to die but instead it seemed like the needed escape hatch I could always turn to during that breaking moment. No one wants to jump out an exit door on an airplane, but we feel better because it is there for that "just in case" emergency. To me, thinking about suicide was the same process. It was the final fallback plan when things reached a point of no return. I would simply say to myself, "If things become terrible then I will just find a way to take my own life. Taking my life will end my suffering and the fear of future suffering." During those moments, I actually accepted that death would be more rewarding than life. Sadly, the thought of ending things brought a sense of peace over me because I believed I had an outlet if things deteriorated with Marley.

When we discuss suicide, I think it is impossible for us to ever really consider that our spouse or friend might actually take his or her own life. When I left one night on our motorcycle, I don't think Jana really thought I was considering the possibility of ending my life. As I walked out for a moment away from my family, Jana thought I was just taking a short break, but I actually took the motorcycle out on the expressway to challenge God. This was the first time in our marriage that I really thought I would never see my wife again in this life. As I stormed out of our apartment, I remember telling her that I loved her and I would be right back. I told her that I just needed a few moments to gather my thoughts and talk to God. Jana was accustomed to this because I had often gone out to "work things out with God." That night, however, I was contemplating meeting God face to face.

A few hundred yards from our apartment is a raging three-lane highway of unforgiving traffic. When you enter that highway in your car, you better prepare for a cutthroat world of aggression or you will be encountering a wreck. Residents wake up every day to reports of motorcyclists being killed in accidents in Bangkok the previous night. The streets of Bangkok can humble the best drivers very quickly because no one cares about your car or your personal space.

The most fascinating thing about the highway in front of our apartment is the motorcycle lane. In that lane you are permitted to go in either direction as long as you stay in your lane. Of course, some motorcyclists will go in either direction against traffic regardless of which lane they are in, but they don't usually survive very long. My first year I actually saw a truck backing up against oncoming traffic because he had missed his turn and did not want to waste time going down to the U-turn bridge. Therefore on the highway, you can either ride along with the three lanes of roaring traffic going in the same direction or you can ride against the traffic, soaring past at sixty miles per hour with only a few inches separating you. Regrettably, this was the perfect place for me to test my courage.

As I left the apartment, I took a back road that was about half-a-mile down from our main street that led to the expressway. My plan was to ride back up the expressway against the traffic. While I was cruising down the back road toward my final bout with God, I was not sure how I would handle the moments before crashing into an oncoming bus. Would I have the courage to take my own life? I often wonder if other people contemplating suicide face this internal struggle of courage. Many people think that killing oneself is a cowardly act in itself, but taking that final plunge is brutal. I was desperate for an escape that appeared easy for me, but in that moment, I had no concern for the future of my wife and child. The only thing occupying my mind as I turned and stopped at the highway intersection was my own pain and suffering. The final escape hatch was there in front of me and once I exited, there would be no return to a life that I believed was too difficult to live. The struggle of my wife raising a child with special needs without a husband was irrelevant because everything in that moment was only about me. This was it—the final end to the pain that had engulfed my life.

Suddenly a bus went roaring by and missed hitting me by just a few inches. The bus masked the high-pitched screaming of my voice and the tears streaming down my face as I anticipated it slamming into me. My mind entered a sense of euphoria after the bus whistled by my ear. While I froze there contemplating entering the roaring highway, I heard a voice speaking to me—a voice that prompted me to *not* turn on the highway and consider the worst of fates. This voice not only changed my course of direction that night but also encouraged me to really embrace the painful struggle I had wrestled with for the past several months.

It was not God, it was not my father, it was not Jana, it was not Marley, and it was not some other supernatural presence. It was my own voice, my own voice of reason. As a believer in God, I believe God could have spoken to me at that moment but he did not because I would not have listened. The voice I heard was *my own voice,* and I think God used that voice to reach me because it was the only one that could grab my attention in my darkest moment. The entire world was dead to me at that moment, but there was still one sound that could prevent my immediate end.

As the bus quickly passed by, the echoing sound of my own

voice rang through my ears. I can only describe it as being a player and a coach at the same moment. For years I have coached basketball and the moment after that bus roared past me, I visualized myself standing and screaming at a player kneeling before me. The coach was screaming down at me and I was fixated on his face. The realization of me simultaneously being both that player and coach broke my fixation on my own selfish desires and made me realize that my life was about more than myself. The coach side of me was yelling, "Stop!" to the player on the side of me kneeling on the floor. Maybe the vision was from my experience of being a player and a coach throughout my life, but for some reason that vision caught my attention. Hearing my own coaching voice scream brought me to a place of realization and salvation; a place of acceptance; a place of peace. The opportunity was there for me to jump through the escape hatch, but my inner coach forced me to push through. The coach brought me back from defeat on that day. He motivated me to focus on accomplishing things that I never thought would be possible with my daughter, wife, and God.

Many of us who have played sports have had that one coach that has changed our lives. On that day, the coach was myself. The coach shouting at me initiated a breakthrough that sent me on a path that has led me to where I am today. The side that my dad must have seen in me when he encouraged me to become a coach saved my life, family, and relationship with God that night in Bangkok.

Immediately I understood that death would not fix the current disaster of my life. It was not Marley, Jana, God, or my absent father hindering me from living the life I thought I deserved, but instead my lack of personal healing. As I stood there on the side of the road crying and profusely sweating, I realized that taking my own life would only rob me of healing my brokenness that had materialized decades before Marley had even entered the picture. As my own voice brought me back from the depths of death, one thing resonated clearly in my mind: death might free me from this temporary suffering that was suffocating my life, but a dead father would be an absent father for Marley. Avoiding that expressway came down to me finding a level of courage that I had never experienced before in my life. Not the courage to test a Bangkok bus, but instead the courage to drive home that night to fix my life. The player inside of me needed a kick in the butt, and thankfully, that coach arrived moments before I considered the decision that would have altered my life for eternity.

Healing is a Slow Process

We often want to fix things quickly and move forward with our busy lives. We are attracted to quick fixes. In today's world we do not have the time or the patience to invest a significant amount of time into anything. In fact, we are so reluctant to invest the required time into something that we often abandon the project before even starting the process. This is what I had done the previous twenty years of my life before that night in Bangkok. Instead of taking the time to embrace the turmoil in my life and work through it, I ignored it because I did not want to waste my precious time. Continuing at the fast pace of life appeared to be a better choice instead of slowing down and taking the steps that I needed to take to work through the issue. For twenty plus years, my approach to problem solving was to suppress and ignore instead of taking the healthy approach of healing and reconciliation.

How often do we see people attempt to conquer an addiction and fail numerous times throughout life? How many years does it take for someone to become an addict? So why do we think a one-time program will enable a person to walk away sober or clean for the remainder of his or her life? The limited success rate is because people don't take the amount of time needed to fight the addiction. However, if we visit a doctor and are diagnosed with cancer, we immediately begin a treatment program to fight the cancer. We are committed to fighting this disease from day one and think of nothing else but victory. Never have I heard of a person telling the doctor, "Oh, so I have prostate cancer. Tell you what, Doc, let me take another year living my life and see if it gets worse." We seem to act quickly when addressing a disease that could take our physical lives, but we routinely procrastinate when faced with emotional issues. Healing takes time and the more we avoid dedicating time to the process, the more likely we will reach a breaking point that will never see reconciliation.

Men especially are reminded by previous generations that openly embracing our faults is not the "manly" approach. The problem is that *we* are the failures in this generation, not women. The amount of men that have abandoned their families is mind-boggling. I believe that one reason for this "father abandonment" is because we cannot embrace our brokenness. We are taught to be tough and lead, but a father that leaves his family is anything but tough. Men, just like women, need support from each other and that involves talking about the issues we normally suppress for our entire lives.

The day after I pondered taking my own life, I was on the phone talking to a father in India that had a son with Down syndrome. For the first time since Marley's birth, I saw a glimmer of hope. What he said was very similar to the information my doctor, family, and friends had previously shared with me about Down syndrome, but he broke through to me on that day when others had not been able to do so. He lifted me from that dark pit of despair with one phrase that started our entire conversation: "I have been where you are right now and survived."

It has been over two years and I have yet to embrace complete healing in my life. The difference today is that the process has started in my life. The hardest step is the first, and the best way to take that step is by finding someone who has been there. Sharing with another person who has encountered the same crippling crisis that you currently face enables you to see the end of the journey. Many fathers are so driven by success, money, and purpose that they refuse to embrace personal healing until it is too late. Embracing personal healing requires fathers to step out and seek the help needed to overcome the despair in their lives. People who have survived the storm will take the time to help others because they understand their agony. Few things are more important in our lives than overcoming pain and suffering. We must take the time to work through these issues and put aside anything else for a significant amount of time.

I wasted the entire first year of my daughter's life by wallowing in my own self-pity and pain. That time is forever stolen from me because I did not use it to heal. Sadly, the remainder of my life was almost taken because I was too proud to embrace my own failures. Loving and caring for our children should be a priority and that begins by overcoming our own faults and failures through healing.

Offer Help, Find Help

Right now you may know someone who is hurting. It might be you or it might be a friend, coworker, or family member. What are you going to do? Are you going to ignore it like we often do when we don't want to confront something in life? Are you going to hope that it will work itself out? This challenge requires you to step out and be a man. Take the first step toward helping yourself or someone else. It is not an easy thing to do because there will be anger, resentment, and confrontation involved. No one likes being told they need help, but the help is more important than the feelings. Maybe it will work out on its own if you never do anything about it. But as leaders we cannot take that chance with people we care about. If you see a problem in your community, then reach out to that person. If that person is you, then take that first step and find the help you need to be the man, husband, and father that God has called you to be.

Yesterday

Sincere fathers should embrace past transgressions to adequately build meaningful relationships with their children.

Chapter 4

Fatherhood Starts with Your Father

Fathers, do not provoke your children to anger by the way you treat them. Rather, bring them up with the discipline and instruction that comes from the Lord. (Ephesians 6:4 NLT)

How does one begin the story of his life? The prominent thought in the Christian circle would be to start any story with God. I do believe that God plays a significant role in my life, but I think the foundation of every boy's story should start with a different character—Dad. If the relationship with our earthly father is damaged, then certain pieces of our relationship with our eternal father might be broken as well. This may be difficult for many to accept because a father may have never been present in their life. When any boy loses his father, he immediately loses an irreplaceable presence in his life. The loss might occur before birth or in the golden years, but regardless of how worthless a father may have been, he is still significant to that boy. When the man that carries the title of *dad* is absent, then the boy will always suffer regardless of his age.

I remember the first time my dad could no longer play catch with me. The superhero I had worshipped for eighteen years became a fragile dying man to me on that day. Playing catch is what ultimately defined me as the person I am today. My father introduced me to the game of baseball before I was born. It was the natural progression in life for me because my father played college baseball, but later chose his family over a baseball career. As soon as my father found out that he was getting another son, ten years after the birth of his last child, he immediately became a full-time coach.

When I was five years old, all of my friends were playing T-ball and I desperately wanted to be on one of the fabulous candy teams (M&M, Milky Way, Almond Joy). The main reason I wanted to sign up was because my friends told me they were given candy after every game. What could be better than combining two great things in life: baseball and candy? I remember approaching my dad about playing T-ball and he told me, "Absolutely not." I will never forget his way of explaining to me that T-ball was not an option for me: "In T-ball a kid hits the ball off a tee; that is not baseball. When they have a pitcher throwing the ball, then you can play." I did not know it then, but my father had already deemed me too good to hit a ball off a tee. My baseball career still started that year, but it consisted of going to the park to practice with my dad while the other kids got to play games and eat candy.

Some people that knew us commented that they believed my father was too hard on me as a child. When I was twelve years old, I hurt my ankle playing pick-up basketball on a Friday night after my dad had specifically told me not to play because we had an important baseball game against the first-place team the next day. I rolled my ankle pretty badly during the basketball game that night so I was icing it when I heard my parents fighting downstairs. My father was adamant I was going to play because it was my responsibility to the team. My mom was telling him that he was crazy and I could hurt my ankle more. As I was lying there listening to them argue, I knew he would make me play because he believed in loyalty. I have met very few veterans that do not value loyalty over most other things, and my father viewed that baseball team as my battalion.

The next day I played, hobbling around the field. The dramatic play of the game was in the last inning when I had a chance to be a hero. As I stood on second base, the next batter—my teammate—got a base hit to center field. I rounded third and looked at the coach, my dad, giving me the stop signal. I didn't care. I was going to be the hero and prove my father wrong. I sprinted home and slid into the catcher as he caught the ball and tagged me. I looked up at the umpire and he yelled, "Out!" When the umpire called me out, I began to cry and everyone thought I was hurt. I grabbed my knee and started rolling around on the ground. My father came down the baseline from third and told me to get up. The umpire told him he thought I was seriously hurt, and I remember another famous father line, "He is not physically hurt, his feelings are hurt because he got tagged out at home. So get up." He jerked me up and dragged me back to the dugout. I heard a gasp through the crowd as I hobbled back to the dugout, my father dragging me along. He whispered to me, "I thought your ankle was hurt, not your knee. If you don't start walking, you are going to get it when we get home." I knew that meant the switch—a tree limb used for discipline—so I stopped hobbling and reluctantly walked with him back to the dugout. We lost the game and the switch was still waiting for me when we got home.

In today's world, my father might stand in front of a judge to discuss child abuse, but in reality he was right. I had lost the game and decided to fake the severity of my injury. Sometimes no one else can see the truth except for Dad. Fathers have a relationship with their children that cannot be duplicated by any other relationship. My mother would have coddled me if my father were not present on that day, and that probably would have led me down a path of more whining and excuse-making in my future years. Fathers have a role that cannot be replaced by a mother—and the same is true for a mother.

The dynamic duo of a mother and a father is important for a reason. A child needs the balance of a caring father and a caring mother. When this influential family model is broken, the child is going to suffer. The traditional family is a necessity for our children. Fathers that leave their children are already taking away a relationship that can never be replaced by anyone else. My father is the reason I am the man I am today. Without his guidance, I know I would have left my child, my wife, and my faith. The model of loyalty I witnessed in him for eighteen years challenged me to work through my own inadequacies and be a father for my daughter. Until fathers accept the vital importance of raising their children, we are going to have broken sons and daughters in this world who will never understand the true meaning of "Dad."

Welcoming Death

He was my catcher and I was his pitcher. By my junior year I was throwing in the mid-eighties, but my dad would still catch me with nothing on but a glove. We would throw for hours in the yard as he would squat and be my critical catcher. This might not seem like a great feat, but he was already over fifty years of age by my senior year of high school. He was the most honest catcher I have ever worked with, but I could not be honest with him on that last day of catch. I could tell something was off from the beginning. I still believe the only reason he wanted to play catch was to prove to me he could overcome cancer.

I started by softly tossing the ball and he quickly became angry. "Stop babying it," he would say. After a few more minutes, I started letting the ball go, and the first true fastball I threw whistled by his ear and hit the car. He wanted to keep going. I was on the verge of tears but I was taught that when your dad tells you to do something, you do it. He told me to throw a curve ball so he could see how my breaking stuff looked. When I threw the ball, it short-hopped him and hit him in the face. He put his glove down and looked up at me with his swollen eye. The pain I saw in his face was not a physical hurt, but the fear of a man that had been defeated. I knew at that moment that things would never be the same and I was losing my father. After that event, we talked very little, and he slowly lost a battle that I always thought he would win.

Anyone who has watched someone battle cancer knows how painful the event can be for the person and their family. I sat and watched my father die while I tried to juggle baseball, college, and a girlfriend. I did what I believed most boys would do when their father becomes terminal: I ran. The pain of watching a man digress to the point of not being able to walk, talk, or move was more than I could handle at eighteen years-of-age. A man that could beat me in a forty-yard dash just a few years earlier had wasted to less than a hundred pounds in twelve months. I started drinking heavily, smoking pot, and spending nights at my girlfriend's house in another town. I avoided my family at all costs. I dropped out of college and hated baseball. I knew my dad was dying and all I wanted to do was numb the pain.

I think as humans we are equipped to handle suffering and pain, but there comes a point when our body shuts down because it is too much to bear. I reached that point on April 11, 1998 when my dad died. Everything we had worked for was gone. Nothing seemed to matter after he was lowered into the grave. Most boys will endure the death (physically or emotionally) of a father at some point in their lives. Odds are we will watch them leave our lives in some way before our own death. I believe when that happens, a small part of us dies with them.

I am a father now. Marley has completely changed my life. How I long to talk to my father about being a father! I try to talk to other fathers but it is not the same as being able to talk to my own father. My dad was a deeply religious man and church was the only place we would spend as much time as a baseball field. He was strict and believed hard work could accomplish anything. He was not perfect but looking back now at those eighteen years together, I realize how much I cherish them. I often think back to my father's guidance when I encounter difficult situations. I think about how he never questioned God regardless of the circumstances, or how he would pick up the man in our town who was mentally disabled and give him a ride anywhere he wanted to go. It did not matter what our plans were at that moment; if someone needed a ride, we would take them. My father was a unique person and he was always there, willing to help me. Even though my father never met my daughter, I know what his advice would be in raising Marley.

> *Well, she has Down syndrome. So what? Look how beautiful she is. I wish you had been this cute when you were that age. It would have made looking at you a little easier. Son, she is now your responsibility. You have to be a father, a hero, and a friend to her all at the same time. Maybe you are heartbroken because she has Down syndrome. You probably sit up at night and cry about it. You are just like your mother. Suck it up. You bust your butt twice as hard to help her. You give her everything you possibly can give her and you work harder to give her more than that. You brought this beautiful girl into this world and don't you think for a second you can give up on her. You stick it out and love her in a way you have never loved anyone else. This world can be a mean and cruel place, so she needs you more than anyone else. This is your time to be a father, and just because she is not what you expected does not mean you can run out on her. She loves you, and it is time you love her like your Creator loves you. God gave you this little angel for a reason, so you give every part of your life to her.*

Every year at Christmas, I look at the small mouth bass that he mounted for me on our annual Tennessee fishing trip. My father would take a week off work every year to take my brother and me river fishing in the Tennessee Mountains. He organized this trip every April because that is what a father should do for his son or daughter. He believed a specific amount of time was needed for a father and a child to be away from mom. The secret of that mounted fish is that he was the one who actually hooked it, but yet he allowed me to reel it in and claim it as mine. That is what a father does. He does not look to glorify himself; he looks to bring glory to his son or daughter and delights in their accomplishments. We need more fathers like this in the world—fathers who put their sons and daughters first, and refuse to walk away when things are not perfect.

How do you do this? First, you have to be there. I know my mother and father had difficult times, but he was committed to his marriage and to his children. You will never have a chance to be a good father if you are an absent father. I believe the majority of problems with young men in this world stem from their lack of strong fathers. My dad believed in responsibility and that is not an easy code to live by in today's world. I had my own doubts and fears when my daughter was born, but you have to be committed for the future of your children. When you choose to leave your son or daughter behind, you are not escaping to an easier life, but instead ruining a life you helped create. We need to be determined to repair broken relationships with our spouses, our families, and our Creator in order to be committed to our role as fathers. Nothing should separate a father/child relationship because being a present dad is essential for our children's future. No boy or girl should have to grow up without a loving father in his or her life.

Hash it Out with Dad

I would like to encourage you with this idea before you proceed to the next chapter. Sit down and write a letter to your father. It does not matter if he is dead, alive, or non-existent. We all have had those times in life when we need to talk to our dad. Feel free and write whatever you want to share with him. Maybe you have never met your father and you want to ask the desperate question of "why?" Maybe he has died and you want to share some things that have happened since his death, or maybe he is alive and you just want to catch up. Write as much or as little as you need to write. The most important aspect of this exercise is for you to be honest and open with your father. Share the things that you are afraid to share at a typical Thanksgiving meal. If we cannot be honest with our father, then how can we ever be honest with ourselves? Once you have finished your letter I encourage you to keep it or give it to him. If your father is not present then put it away for your future son or daughter for after they enter adulthood. Maybe you will never have children, but if you do, consider sharing your heartfelt letter to your dad with your child one day because it could deeply enrich your relationship.

Chapter 5

Fathers Must Confront Past Evils

If anyone causes one of these little ones—those who believe in me—to stumble, it would be better for them if a large millstone were hung around their neck and they were thrown into the sea.
(Mark 9:42 NIV)

Note: the events in this chapter are true however names and places have been changed.

It was called "doctor." The only doctor game I knew was a board game called Operation (Milton Bradley), but there was no board game present when an older boy introduced me to this game. This game, "doctor" would change my life and set me on a course of broken relationships for the next twenty years.

It began with a trip. Most of my childhood took place in my father's hometown, but frequently we would take a forty-five minute car ride to visit my grandmother in my mother's hometown. These trips led me to a new group of friends that I would see about twice a month. I was one of the younger kids in the group and I wanted to become significant in this new group of friends. The older boys I hung out with dominated the group and I was constantly looking for things to do while my mother visited my grandmother. The group gradually welcomed me, but I was still viewed as an outsider to them. Many of their conversations revolved around their hometown and school, so rarely did I feel like I belonged. The guys eventually started to accept me as one of the gang after several months of visiting, and finally endorsed my membership by introducing me to smoking cigarettes. I could not suppress the excitement I felt when I got to sit with the guys and smoke cigarettes. At that moment, I thought, "This is what it feels like to be cool." I was certain that now I was one of them.

The darkness of evil began to materialize one afternoon when I was alone with one of the leaders of the group. He was the oldest boy, and the one that approved of newcomers before they were accepted by the entire group. Of course, I was with him every chance I got because I was desperate to be popular. The concept of *being liked* became the downfall to my understanding of what was right and wrong. These guys were supposedly my friends and I wanted to do anything I could to be approved by them.

One afternoon, I stayed with the leader of the group while the other boys were out playing. He had stolen some wine coolers and we were drinking while watching television. He told me he had gotten a new pornographic movie from a friend and he wanted to watch it with me. As we were watching it he started telling me about a game he had learned called "doctor." He was at a stage in life where only sexual desires controlled his thoughts and actions, but I was at a stage in life where acceptance was the thing that mattered most. We kept drinking and he started showing me the game.

He explained that the game consisted of him acting like something was hurt then I would touch it and massage away the pain. It started simple enough with him saying his back hurt or his arm hurt. Uneasiness crept into my mind as I rubbed his shoulders, but I suppressed it with all of my might. Peer acceptance was dominating my mind and I was going to be accepted. As we continued, I could not understand why I was the doctor every time and he was the patient. The reality began to sink in as he explained to me that my turn would come after he felt better. His third request was leading me to touch something I knew was unacceptable. I started to fidget and tell him I had never touched someone there before. He said it was ok and he would walk me through it. Tears began streaming down my face and I pleaded with him to stop. Regardless of your opinions or thoughts on sexual fulfillment, I hope you would agree that an older boy should never have control over a younger child. The situations we confront in life that we know are wrong are often overshadowed by a twisted view of acceptance. That day, my "friend" cared more about his instant sexual gratification than the damage he was doing to a young child's mind for the remainder of his life.

While I started to slide away, he pulled down his underwear to expose himself. I told him that I was not sure what he wanted me to do and he asked me if I wanted to be part of the group. I told him of course and he immediately grabbed my hand and put it where he wanted. I stared at him—not moving at all and in a state of shock for a long time. I was frightened and I could feel the evil building in my stomach to nauseating proportions. We had done some dreadful things before, but this was a different realm of shame from which I felt I would never return. His next statement still haunts my mind even to this day, "Are you retarded or something? Move your hand before I hit you." I never returned to the group after that day and my official membership in the club was forever severed.

There are events in our lives that shape the very existence of who we are as fathers. These events, whether good or evil, are important for us to not only embrace but share with others regardless of the pain these events might cause. I am sharing this horrific event to help you gain a better understanding of my first true encounter with evil and how it shaped my ultimate decision twenty-plus years later. When an event like this happens in our lives that is extremely devastating, our initial reaction is to suppress it in order to continue life. Our body uses this survival mechanism in order to cope with the horrific event. My mind has often suppressed this event amazingly well, and I will forget it even occurred until a nightmare strikes me during the night. This coping approach has not been beneficial for my family or me. Certainly there are times we must psychologically flee from evil encounters, but true healing needs to come from vulnerability. Concealing traumatic experiences in our lives might assist us in handling the situation at the moment, but I believe if these issues are never addressed, our future lives will be dramatically affected.

This event also sent me down a path of perverted relationships with other women before I met my wife, Jana. What I thought was acceptable and pleasurable was actually a twisted view of sexual fulfillment. That one experience opened a door to sexual involvement that I am deeply ashamed of and regret. That afternoon I was used to fulfill a desire and that transformed me into continuing unhealthy sexual experiences with others. It was never a forceful act for me after that encounter, but it was certainly something that should never be present in a person's life. Not confronting and dealing with that dreadful act when it happened propelled me into relationships that were unhealthy for others and for me.

I am also sharing this because I think events like this happen very often in our society but are hidden away. These experiences are not discussed or shared in the family circle so we "sweep it under the rug," and it becomes even more detrimental to our sons and daughters. This one event from my childhood unwillingly altered my perspective regarding trusting others, sexual meaning, and separation anxiety. Unfortunately it took the birth of my own daughter, over twenty years later, for me to realize that this catastrophe had not only perverted my sexual appetite but also altered my worldview.

We often excuse evil as something God "unfairly let happen" to our children instead of mending the wound. This leads to a life of resentment, not healing. True healing and mending is what our soul craves, not understanding. We must realize that God despises evil and when our soul is broken, God mourns. For the past twenty years God has been the center of my anger because I was suppressing this horrific event. Inadequate healing and reconciliation led me to believe that the unhealthy relationships I had with my family, friends, and Creator were normal.

Forever Changed

Tragic days like the story described above are examples of wickedness stealing the innocence of childhood. People are capable of accomplishing beautiful things for the good of society but also, unfortunately, of inflicting hurtful acts upon one another. The choices we make and carry out every day dictate the eternal imprint we make on our society. We must approach life with a sense of compassion while battling selfish desires. Regrettably, a large percentage of despicable acts involve children because they are the most defenseless group in our society. The pain and shame I encountered that day has altered every single relationship in my life since that event. Only through hours of counseling and conflict have I been able to embrace the idea of a healthy sexual relationship.

Psychologists constantly remind us that children are extremely vulnerable during their development because that is when they are forming their beliefs, worldviews, and visions of life. The domino effect of that event led me to participate in the same dreadful self-satisfying acts that were forced upon me. The only escape I felt was entering relationships that could meet my own self-gratification. Relationships were viewed as stepping stones toward my overall success which led me to abusing God, my family, my friends, and my significant others. That day introduced me to a world of using other people for my gain instead of viewing people as an equal creation of God.

Of course, many people in our society don't care—and that is the most disturbing aspect of this entire story. People are raised in an environment that focuses on the "me first," and if hurting others is a step in that process then they are more than willing to do it. The ideology of putting others first is becoming a more foreign thought for people. Hurting children is still frowned upon in our culture, but we have become more concerned with rehabilitating the criminal than caring for the victim. This approach only leads to more torment as the victim seeks to reconcile his or her life while the culprit searches for another victim. Could these events that involve hurting children physically or emotionally be prevented in our society? Maybe, but the focus on prevention cannot be a reason to minimize our need of responses to victim healing.

As I close this chapter about this atrocious event in my life, I want to stop and challenge you for a moment as fathers. First, be strong enough to ask the difficult question when someone in your family seems aloof. Look for signs that can help you determine if a child in your family is being abused. There are numerous resources available that can guide you in helping a child. The shame and disgust I felt from that afternoon sent me down a path of denial and suppression. Becoming withdrawn, having outbursts of anger, self-mutilation, and attempts to run away are just a few of the things I used to do to manage the pain. Of course, these warning signs do not always implicate sexual abuse, but the worst approach is the approach we most often take with our family members—and that is ignoring the evidence.

Second, embrace the problem and handle it with compassion while discussing it with your family. Facing the problem might lead to anger, broken relationships, and police involvement, but remember you are trying to protect a child. Start with the immediate family and approach the subject as a humble caring family member. Don't accuse, but instead share your concerns based on the behavior you are observing. Bring in a counselor if you suspect sexual abuse by adults or other children. Talking to an outside party in a confidential setting can often enable a child to share his or her darkest thoughts without the fear of judgment. Do what your heart guides you to do. Don't second-guess yourself but rather consider acting on your "gut feeling." Even if you are completely wrong, it is better to be embarrassed than let sexual abuse continue.

Finally, take the time to help the victim heal. Instead of trying to solve it quickly, take the long approach and mend a person's soul. We usually want to immediately blame someone and work to instantly fix the problem. That technique will not work with victims of sexual abuse. This event has been something I have wrestled with for a significant amount of my life. It altered my childhood, my role as a husband, and ultimately my failure as a father. You must stay connected with the victim for many years and offer friendship at anytime, day or night. It will be a difficult road, but it will be rewarding when you venture through the process together, victim and friend, to reach the final stage of forgiveness. Overcoming malicious events in our lives will take family, counseling and God to find true reconciliation.

Restoring Our Souls as Fathers

Everyone in life experiences a time when they are hurt and when they hurt someone else. Writing this book forced me to travel back in my past and deal with the incident. It was difficult, but something that needed to be done for me to move forward. The problem is that I faced a dilemma while revis-

iting this hideous event in my past. I could continue to hold on to the anger and hatred I had for the boy who abused me or I could embrace forgiveness. After several weeks, I finally concluded the only way I could move forward was to offer forgiveness. This forgiveness could only come through my relationship with God because of the pain I personally felt from the event. But sometimes forgiveness is a process. It is easy to say you forgive someone but never reach true reconciliation. True forgiveness can be extremely difficult and I hope you will try to find that peace. It might take days, months, or years of forgiving someone to finally reach that point of acceptance, but the process will be life-changing.

I want to challenge you to take a moment now and forgive someone who has truly hurt you in life. This is an extremely difficult thing to do, but anger that continues to fester in your soul damages your ability to be a loving father. Take a five-minute break from the world right now and clear your mind. Call on God for guidance and support while embarking on this difficult task. Do as Jesus did and forgive that person that hurt you. I found a quiet room and audibly said, "I forgive [the person]," several times while sitting peacefully for about five minutes. As stated above, this might need to be a routine you do numerous times to find that forgiveness. Regardless, take the time needed to find forgiveness because forcing yourself to forgive that person will free you from the yoke of resentment that is affecting your everyday relationships.

Chapter 6

A Righteous Slap Is Often Needed for Guidance

Then Jesus entered the Temple and began to drive out the people selling animals for sacrifices. He said to them, "The Scriptures declare, 'My Temple will be a house of prayer,' but you have turned it into a den of thieves." (Luke 19:45-46 NLT)

My mother and I did not have an extremely close relationship during my childhood. There was always a distance between us that I cannot explain. It was not a neglectful act, but instead a situation in which I preferred to spend time with my father than my mother. I believe this is typical of most boys because of the human connection I discussed in the early chapters. So many things would have been absent in my life with only a mother. My father taught me baseball, how to fish, and everything else a young boy craves during his developmental years from his dad. My mother preferred cooking and cleaning, which never appealed to me during childhood, or actually now. The unique closeness I felt with my father was not replicated with my mom until years after my father's death. I loved her and she loved me, but those secret moments that I shared with my father were not present with my mother during my childhood.

Discipline was usually left to my father. I cannot recall a single time when my mother would grab a paddle and give me a good dose of corporal punishment. Instead, my mother would use a simple sentence that would send my day into complete dismay, "Just wait till your father gets home!" Honestly I probably heard that phrase over a thousand times during my formative years. My mother would get so angry that her face would turn crimson red and I could see the desire in her eyes to spank me, but she would always take a deep breath and hit me with that disastrous statement. I think she began to realize that the agony of me waiting for my father to get home at six every evening was far worse than any punishment she could facilitate before his arrival. I remember sitting in my room and thinking about how painful the punishment would be when my father would arrive and paddle my butt. In fact, one time I put on about eight pairs of underwear to help absorb the impact of the paddle. My father started to catch on when I seemed to be moving very little during each strike. He told me to pull down my pants and was astonished to see my creative thinking. I am not sure if he was proud at that moment or angry about my sneaky manipulation. Regardless, that day was when the switch was introduced to me. The switch took the place of the paddle and the day of padding my pants with underwear on were over because the switch always got the bare butt offering.

Looking back on it now, the moment of discipline was never as bad as I would have imagined it before he got home from work. "Guess what your son did today," became a precursor to my father slowly climbing the steps up to my room with a paddle or switch in his hands. This routine became fairly common during my elementary years, but things drastically changed one morning that forever altered the way I viewed my mother. You can only push a mom so far before you endure the ramifications of her "snapping."

My mother was a first grade teacher assistant until she retired a few years ago. The woman I knew as the passive caretaker spent numerous hours helping children that needed a little extra attention. I quickly realized that the job of a teacher assistant was far from glamorous. With very little recognition and the numerous tasks required of her, my mother still enjoyed the job of caring for horrendous little children. If a woman were ever born for a specific job then my mother would be a perfect example of that anomaly. Unfortunately for me, every morning we would ride to school together as she would go to teach and I would go to learn. Since my mother worked at the school, I became a regular fixture on campus before and after school. I would always go in early with her and come back late with her most days. Even when I started middle school, I would ride with her to the elementary school were she worked. I would then catch a bus to the middle school and then climb back on the bus every afternoon returning to the elementary school to get a ride home with my mom. Every time I got into trouble, my mom would be the first to learn of my misbehavior through the great rumor mill of teacher gossip. By lunchtime my mom knew of the incident, the people involved, and had planned to inform my father about it when we got home. Hopping in the car most afternoons was met with, "I heard what you did in Mrs. ______ class today". It was impossible for me to "get away" with anything with my teachers because every misstep was seen as a reason to inform my mother that I had misbehaved that day.

As I got older, I became more defiant and embraced a newfound courage I had found among my peers. This sense of invincibility led to a dangerous misstep one morning on the ride to work with "dear ol' mom." Middle school gave me a new awareness of how tough I thought I was and how I was ready to challenge this woman that deferred to passing on punishment to my father every afternoon.

Music was the defiant weapon I chose because my parents despised the "rap music" movement that was happening throughout the country. Like my teachers at school, my parents associated this music with gangs and violence, so all possible resources were used to deter my classmates and me from listening to rap music. Of course, this only added fuel to the fire and we adamantly pursued opportunities to listen to the artists that "understood our struggles" (like stated earlier, I was raised in a small town in the South). The necessity to quietly sneak around and defy our parents in private led me to step up and make a statement one dreary morning while riding to school.

She always held the steering wheel at ten and two and drove with two feet. The most cautious driver I knew was always chauffeuring me to school every morning. My mother has never received a speeding ticket and still frequently reminds me that she has never been in a wreck. Even now at the age of thirty-five, I still tell my mother that she should not drive with two feet but she immediately responds by asking, "How many tickets have you had?"

When we embarked on our journey to school that morning, everything in the car was already prepared for the trip. Seatbelts, mirrors, and the radio were all properly adjusted before pulling out of our driveway and were not to be tampered with during our fifteen-minute ride to school. But little did my mom know this ride would be different and change our relationship forever.

Radio station 104.1—the great country station of the time—was our morning music. I despised country music for no other reason than that my parents liked it. Of course now, I enjoy a little bit of classic country music, but during those early years I believed it was a torturous blend of rednecks and hillbillies. As we pulled out on the two-lane road by our house I reached for the radio knob and quickly flipped the station to 102. That was the station that we all tuned into when our parents were not around. 102 played the most recent pop and rap music of our generation. Of course, that station was banned from being played in our car but this was my day of defiance. Besides, my mom was such a cautious driver that I knew she would not dare change the station while our car was racing down the street. This small victory was mine, and I could not wait to share the news at school and gain those valuable popularity points that I needed. Being part of the group was the only thing that mattered and "my boys" would be impressed by the way I had "handled" my mom that glorious morning.

"Jack Jr., please turn the station back to 104," was the only thing my mother said as she calmly kept her eyes on the road. I ignored her and looked out the window. I knew she was caught in a difficult position because she valued car safety. She was the type of mom that would stick her arm across me when she had to stop suddenly. Even though I had on a seat belt, she somehow believed that her holding my body in place while we crashed would somehow keep me in the seat. Looking back now on that simple act of holding me in my seat helps me realize how much my mother actually cared about me during those years. But this was my day and this outdated woman needed to understand the genius of rap music and my newfound independence. Then it happened quickly and suddenly while I was looking out the window. That terrible country music came blaring back across the speakers. I was shocked. Did something happen to radio station 102? As I turned back to look at the radio, I caught a glimpse of my mother's hand going back to the steering wheel. She had actually done it. She had reached over and turned the station back to 104. I was furious. She had ruined my perfect plan and stolen the story I would share with my crew about how I had opposed my mother and her terrible music choices. I felt defeated and humiliated. I was in middle school and she should respect what I wanted to listen to and when I wanted to listen to it. Then it happened. I am not sure why it happened because I had been taught to never use profanity, but it transpired anyway. I looked at my mother with defiance and stated, "I don't want to listen to this ****** ****** station!"

It came like a flash of lightening. Looking back now I am not sure how she moved so quickly. My mother always seemed to be passive and methodical in everything she did, but not this time. She slapped me across the face with such vigor that the blow would have honored Muhammad Ali. My head went crashing into the window and I felt the sting of a thousand little bees attacking my face. The surprise of this woman striking me, who always passed on the punishment to someone else, made it hurt even more. With my dad, I had a moment to absorb the pain that was coming, but this attack was a complete shock and awe campaign. The tears and snot were gushing full stream now and the awkwardness I felt from the radio station battle was insignificant compared to the waterfall of embarrassment I had felt. Slowly I looked back at her, and I could see the anger in her face as she was also crying. Quietly, like a silent whisper, she instructed me to never use the Lord's name in vain around her again. The remainder of the trip consisted of me crying with my head against the window and my mother gripping the steering wheel like it was a wild animal.

Nothing else was ever said about the incident for the remainder of my childhood because the message had been delivered. Even now some twenty years later, when I ask my mother about it, she smiles and states she has no recollection of the incident. Maybe she does not remember the slap, or maybe she has chosen to forget it. Regardless, it has been etched in my memory as one of those events you will never forget. That morning I was ashamed of being whacked by my forty-year-old mother, but something else happened that I never admitted to anyone else. I gained a respect for my mother that I had never before experienced. My mother, the quiet, non-combative person in my life, did what needed to be done at that moment to correct my behavior. I deserved to be slapped for what I had said to her and she obliged me by slapping my face. Of course, she was angry and she reacted without thinking, but it was the correct retribution for my actions. After that moment, I continued to use profanity, but never in front of my mother. In fact, even now, when I let a word slip here or there, I feel a little guilt in my heart. Strangely the guilt is not from my commitment to my religious beliefs, but rather the guilt of disappointing my mother. I got a dose of reality and truth that morning in the car. It took me many years later to understand the significance of that moment, but now I am thankful that the woman who would give up an arm to save my life was willing to do the one thing she hated the most: discipline me.

We Need People Today to Speak Truth Like My Mother

Over the past year, I have spent an enormous amount of time on the phone with various families, counselors, and friends discussing aspects of my depression. During those times, we would talk about the difficulties I was experiencing trying to adjust to having a daughter with a disability. Encouragement and positive feedback were plentiful and I began to see the joy that can be experienced by having a child that was a little different. Of course, these phone conversations would include the difficult times that were to be expected raising a child with special needs, but most of the conversations were uplifting and encouraging. About eight months after Marley's birth, I got a phone call from a friend that took our routine conversations in a different direction. It was a conversation that I needed and it took me back to that life-changing day when my mother adamantly stated through a slap that she was not going to listen to rap music.

Thomas began the conversation by asking me how things were going. I immediately launched into a gloomy description of my heartaches and fears about Marley. Of course, we had ventured down this path before and he quietly listened as I shared my lengthy update about how miserable my life had become. After about twenty minutes, I was expecting him to reassure me that everything was going to be ok like he had done numerous times in the past. Usually he would offer some insight about dealing with depression and we would talk about how this life experience was affecting my relationship with God. But like my mother, Thomas realized that I was going down a road that was detrimental and that immediate intervention was required for me to change course. He began his feedback by simply saying, "That is enough." I remember trying to interrupt him after that statement with a halfhearted, "Huh?" Thomas then launched into a lecture that reminded me of a man that had left me through death many years earlier.

> *That is enough. I have listened to you complain and whine for the past eight months. I know this is hard and not what you expected, but now is the time to start being a father. None of us are prepared for fatherhood, and you are no different because your daughter has Down syndrome. Maybe Marley is not exactly what you envisioned but none of our children are what we picture when we learn our wife is pregnant. You need to stop this and be a father. Not only that, you need to start being a husband again. Your wife has been patiently waiting on you for the past several months to be the man she married ten years ago. How long are you going to do this? It is time you suck it up and embrace this job of fatherhood. I know you are hurting and I know you are angry, but this self-loathing needs to cease. You are starting to sound pathet-*

> *ic. Having Marley is not the worst thing that can happen to you and it's time to start showing some appreciation for this beautiful girl. I don't want to hear it anymore. When we talk from now on, it is going to be positive and not some depressing sob story. Man up and get some help. Find a counselor or therapist and get this crap sorted out. Eight months is enough time for a man to pull his life back together and that is what you should start doing. I love you and I care about you but this is becoming ridiculous. Marley requires a loving father who will protect her. Jana hungers for a husband who will start caring for her again. I know your desire is to be a better man than you were a year ago, so get it together.*

After about a minute of silence, I told Thomas I had to go and hung up the phone. It was impossible for him to call me back because I was in Bangkok and he was in Tennessee. I had been walking around the school soccer field during the entire conversation so I decided to stop and sit down. I began to cry, not because of my dark depression, but because I knew Thomas was right. It was time to move forward and embrace this role that I had been called to fill.

It is our duty as men, husbands, and fathers to find one or two genuine friends who have the green light to slap us with the brutal truth when it is necessary. Currently, I have three people in my life that fill that role—no-nonsense guys that can look through the junk in my life and see the true demons tormenting me. Guys who are not afraid to "step on my toes" by addressing the deficiencies in my life. These friends are an essential support group because we live in a society that encourages us to live free and do whatever we want. That might be a good approach for some people but not for fathers. Fathers cannot just do what they want. Fathers must be committed to the future of their children and that means sometimes you do what is best for your family and not for you. Of course, there is always an easier path and it tempts us during the dark times of fatherhood. In fact, we often teeter between choosing the bright lights of freedom or driving home from work night after night to our demanding family. But the future of our children depends on the choices we make when those temptations come knocking on our doors. This is not about what I want; this is about what my child needs.

The argument of being a successful part-time dad is ridiculous. Look at the divorce rate in our country that suggests half of the fathers reading this book are part-time dads. No statistic or researcher can convince me that a part-time father can successfully impact his child's life in the same way as a full-time father. You may have excuses and legitimate reasons explaining why you are not living in the same house as your son or daughter. It may not even be a choice for you to be in the same house as your child. But we have to fix this problem—and the best way to do that is to be there for your baby boy or girl every day.

There are days I want to leave it all. The crying, the washing dishes, the watching cartoons, the nagging wife, and the constant attention Marley requires from the moment I walk in the door—it can drive any father toward "brighter" options. But this is my family and my child. I have a responsibility that requires me to stick it out even when it is not "fun." There are days that I don't want to hear the truth. This book is filled with my flaws and choices that sent my life spiraling out of control. But this story is rooted in a foundation of accountability—and that can be achieved through the men you ask to support you during your journey. Some days I try to avoid these essential men in my life because I know the slap of reality is coming. But I need it—and they find me.

When I think about that morning my mother slapped me, I often reflect on the story of Jesus and the rich man that I have read many times in the Bible. The rich man has dutifully led a good and decent life by keeping all of God's commandments. So, he decides to ask Jesus what more must he do to inherit the kingdom of God. Jesus confronts him with a slap of reality of what he is missing. Jesus knows the one thing that the man cannot give up—because it means more to him than following Christ. In the same way, we are asked to give up the one thing that most of us struggle with giving up in order to raise our children—constant freedom. That all-in commitment is the hardest thing for us to sacrifice, but the reward of raising a stable son or daughter definitely trumps everything else.

> *"Teacher," the man replied, "I've obeyed all these commandments since I was young." Looking at the man, Jesus felt genuine love for him. "There is still one thing you haven't done," he told him. "Go and sell all your possessions and give the money to the poor, and you will have treasure in heaven. Then come, follow me. "At this the man's face fell, and he went away sad, for he had many possessions. Jesus looked around and said to his disciples, "How hard it is for the rich to enter the Kingdom of God!" This amazed them. But Jesus said again,*

> *"Dear children, it is very hard to enter the Kingdom of God. In fact, it is easier for a camel to go through the eye of a needle than for a rich person to enter the Kingdom of God! (Mark 10:20-25 NLT)*

We can give up money, jobs, hobbies, weekends, toys, and numerous other things, but the sacrifice of being a full time involved father is difficult. I am not only speaking to men that have left their families. I was a non-existent father for the first year of Marley's life even though I slept in the same bed as my wife, helped with chores, and ate dinner every night with my family. The "spending time factor" must be a priority for us to be a full-time dad.

What must you do to be a great father? First you have to stay with your family and force yourself to spend quality time with your children. *But, I want to ________.* That "but" is the problem in our lives. *But I love another woman. But I want to spend time doing other things. But I want to be single again. But my daughter has a disability. But I want to have the freedom to travel. But I want a life free of responsibility.* Just like in the encounter that Jesus had with the young rich man, the question is *what is really important to you?* Are your personal desires aligned with the future well-being of your child? If not, then we have failed as fathers for the future generation. If we can find **accountability partners** who can hold us liable and bring us back to the necessity of raising our children even in our weakest moments, then maybe we can start a movement of commitment instead of abandonment in our society. My daughter needs me, and if it takes a close friend slapping me every day to help me realize that, then I welcome the tears and the snot.

Accountability, Accountability, Accountability

You need at least two in my opinion—two close friends that you respect and trust. These two people are going to be your accountability partners. I have found that it works better for me not to reciprocate the responsibility. What I mean is that for the guys that are my accountability partners, I do not also hold them accountable for their lives. This helps us avoid a give and take process. These guys are there for me and they listen to me, without thinking about sharing their own problems. Maybe that is selfish, but that is what I need and they understand the agreement. They have their own friends that they share their burdens with but not me. Now you need to find them. Make a list of your top twenty friends and start whittling down the list. I would have at least one person that is quite a bit older than you for the mentorship factor—someone that has "been there and done that." I chose my guys based on trust. Who would I be comfortable sharing my darkest secrets with and trust that they would keep it secret while offering me guidance?

Finally, give them the green light. Tell them to slap you when necessary. For some of you, that might be a physical act, but for most of you it will probably be a verbal lashing. Many of us have had a coach that could call us out when we were screwing around at practice. We secretly loved it when he/she would "get on our butt" and not let anything slide. Unfortunately many of us no longer have that influential person in our lives as adults. As men we need some proper butt kicking and that is the main responsibility of these friends that we have asked to join us through life. Start forming your "inner circle" and be sure to contact them when you are facing doubts, fears, and temptations. If routine meetings do not work for you (it did not work for me) then tell them to check up on you from time to time. Also make sure it is ok for you to contact them at any time, day or night. You don't want to be contemplating a major decision in life and wonder if it is too late in the night to call your closest friend.

Chapter 7

My Search for God Started in Mongolia

And after my body has decayed, yet in my body I will see God. I will see him for myself. Yes, I will see him with my own eyes. I am overwhelmed at the thought. (Job 19:26-27 NLT)

Is there a God? It seems like an easy question, one any child could answer. Why are four little words so important for our life, humanity, and death? The answer to this question has caused wars, family divisions, child abandonment, senseless murders, and various other inhumane injustices throughout the history of civilizations. So, why even enter the discussion of the existence of God if the end result can only be disagreement? I believe our belief or lack of belief in God is the foundation of every decision we make in this life. Our view of God ultimately constructs our values, choices, education, profession, and approaches to navigate this journey called life. My entire worldview begins with this basic question—is there a God? Until you can decide your answer to this question, your life will be a shifting vessel with no clear course or destination.

Is there a God? "I don't know"—I am sure that is not the answer you were expecting after the opening paragraph. Allow me to clarify: I *believe* there is a God on most days of my life. I cannot prove to you that there is a God in the same way that you cannot prove to me that there isn't a God. I have heard preachers and atheists that adamantly state we can prove that God exists or doesn't exist. If I could prove to you that God existed then where would be the need for faith?

Faith is not based on me showing you a visual God, but instead believing in something we cannot see. Unfortunately, our "advanced" society views the "belief in something we cannot see" as a person's meager attempt to have a crutch when dealing with the realities of life. After my journey, I would argue that the absence of a belief in God leads us to the destruction of our society because we cannot find the purpose for our lives. Finding this so-called purpose must be an important dilemma that you are determined to answer. This internal struggle of finding purpose is a hunger we must satisfy to be a meaningful father.

New School, New Acceptance

As I stated in the opening, my father became terminally ill during my senior year of high school and died my freshman year of college. At that time I was on a baseball scholarship at a university in North Carolina. One night while running at school, I started to seriously question why I was four hours away from home while my father was slowly dying. In a year, my father had gone from an extremely athletic fifty-year-old man to someone who could not get out of bed, chew his own food, go to the bathroom, or utter a single sound. That next morning, I told my college coach that I was leaving school to be with my father. He tried to convince me to take a leave of absence, but I told him I needed to quit. This went against everything my father believed in, but walking away from that college was one of the best decisions I ever made in my life.

The next few weeks I watched my father die and helped my mother the best I could with the arrangements. Late one night as I was smoking a joint in my car, I started thinking about what would happen to my father once he died. For my entire life, he had dragged me to church to worship this being that promised an afterlife. So I played the part and followed along with the other kids in going to Sunday school, being in Christmas pageants, and pretending to pay attention during long sermons. Suddenly I understood that in a few days my father's "faith" would either be justified through eternity, or would become a worthless dedication to a non-existent being. My chest became very heavy at that moment and all at once, I could not breathe—it was my first panic attack. This question of God's existence—one that meant less to me than thoughts about my next meal prior to this moment—was a frightening dilemma I needed to solve. My father's life was ending, but his eternal life would be determined in a few days when he took his final breath. Gasping for air, I swung open the car door and realized that I needed to confront the fear and find an answer before I became like my father.

I started the fall semester of 1998 at a Christian university in Tennessee. My youth minster had attended the same school and he recommended trying it for a semester. At the time, he believed

I was being called into the ministry, but I had another agenda on my mind. If there was a God, then this school would be a place I could find "him"—a place where young men and women dedicated their lives to serve regardless of where they were called. If I could not find God at this school, then in my mind he obviously did not exist.

The problem I encountered on the first day at college was that all of these students were foundationally-based Christians who were already committed followers. When they filled out their applications, they meant what they said about their commitment to Jesus Christ. Unfortunately I lied on seventy-five percent of my application because I knew that was the only way I would be accepted into the school.

Do you drink?
No (I drank on weekends)

Do you use tobacco?
No (I just dip everyday)

Do you believe in saving sex for marriage?
Yes (Who is a virgin entering college?)

Do you know Jesus Christ as your personal savior?
Yes (I can recite some facts)

These were the correct answers that I gave to be accepted, but they were the exact opposite of my actual life. It became clear in the first two weeks that I was an outcast in my own university. While I was treading water to survive, the believers were doing a perfect spiritual butterfly stroke up and down the biblical pool. Everything I thought was "cool" was quickly viewed as sinful and (my favorite word) "pagan." I had a few friends, but I had a better chance of being recruited by the division one-football team down the road than finding a grounded Christian girl to date me. It appeared most girls at JBC were looking for husbands and not boyfriends. That became a huge obstacle for me because I was looking for a girlfriend and not a future wife.

After the first semester I was on academic probation (1.2 GPA), work-study probation (did not meet weekly hour requirements), athletic probation (could not play baseball that coming spring), and conduct probation (purchasing alcohol with a fake ID). The dean at the time still reminds me today that I was the only student to achieve full probation status in a single semester. The only saving grace I had to continue school in the spring was that my father had just died from cancer and I was viewed as a lost soul needing direction. The college disciplinary board gave me one more chance to figure out my life and calling, basically follow the rules, or that would be the end of my journey to find God at their university.

Yurt "Ger"

During the Christmas break of my sophomore year, I traveled to Mongolia to work with a missionary that had grown up in my hometown. This was my first time traveling to Asia and experiencing a culture different from my own. We spent two weeks in Ulaanbaatar and one week in a town named Red Mouth, which was a twelve-hour drive from the city. No electricity, no running water, and twenty degrees below zero were some of the luxuries I encountered during that week in Red Mouth.

We traveled to Red Mouth because the missionary I was working with had built a relationship with this isolated town over the previous six years. Every summer he would travel to Red Mouth to help the community improve education, teach them about nutrition, and share the love of Christ. The main project he assisted them in accomplishing was repairing a school for their village. Traveling during the winter break was a new experience for him, and when we arrived after a twelve hour trip, the village community was ecstatic to have the "Christian foreigners" visiting them during the harsh winter.

We stayed with a Mongolian family in their *Ger*, a one-room felt-lined tent, and discussed the upcoming summer. The missionary I assisted had been staying with this family for several years and had developed a unique relationship with the father. The family viewed the missionary as one of their own and embraced him like any other relative visiting their home. Spending a night with this family of four opened my eyes to a life that was very different from my own.

The last night before we left Red Mouth, I woke to a creaking noise. I assumed that it was very late at night because I remember seeing everyone asleep as I looked around the room. I quickly realized that the noise I heard was not from the animals outside, but rather it was from the father and mother. I guess the week of having guests constantly in their tent had interfered enough with their love life that they had no choice but to try the "quiet sex" route. Either that, or they did not care about being heard (I never got to ask). A nauseous feeling began to creep up in my stomach as the love-making became more intense. I could not get up and leave because that would have been more embarrassing than hearing their rumble in the sheets so I waited out the torment.

As the grunting became louder, I rolled over on my side and began to cry. For some unexplainable reason, the first sexual experience I ever had entered my mind and I began to think about the purpose of my life. For the past year I had been living a lie, and was supposedly trying to "seek God." I had rebelliously broken every rule that could restrict me. My father was dead, I was failing at school, and here I was in the middle of Mongolia listening to an old married couple have sex. My life had no meaning or purpose and my existence was numb and aimless.

Once the couple finished and drifted off to sleep, I slowly got up and went outside to absolute darkness and snow-covered ground. We had slept in our clothes because of the frigid temperatures, so I was able to stand outside to reflect a few moments. As I stood outside freezing while looking at the stars, I realized I had wasted enough time living an unproductive life. In the snow, I dropped to my knees and swore to find an answer. At that moment, I cried out to God and said, "If you exist, then please reveal yourself to me." Nothing magical happened at that moment, nor did God appear to me in a vision. However, one simple thing transpired that gave me a glimpse into something beyond this earthly world. A counselor or psychologist might excuse it as a mental reaction to freeing myself from pain, but for the first time, a moment of peace covered my soul such that I had not felt since before my first encounter with evil several years earlier. I believe the peace that comforted my soul that night was the breath of God revealing himself to me. Skeptics will argue that the peace I felt was the body's reaction to the cleansing process, but I know something on that frigid night entered my life for the first time, and gave me a peace that can never be adequately explained in words. That night, I left the hopelessness of broken relationships there in the snow and reentered the Ger with a mission to start a new life with my Creator.

Finding that Purpose

You need to figure out if there is a God. We often avoid this question when asked by other people because it scares us. We don't want to take the time to investigate the issue of God so we just ignore it. We fill our time with other things so the dilemma of God is not a pressing issue. The only thing I want you to do before reading the next chapter is to be honest with yourself. Will you genuinely consider the answer to the question of whether or not God exists? There are no other strings attached to this challenge. My hope is that you will just consider seeking an answer.

Chapter 8

The Wife Who Guided Me to Fatherhood

May your fountain be blessed, and may you rejoice in the wife of your youth. A loving doe, a graceful deer—may her breasts satisfy you always, may you ever be intoxicated by her love. (Proverbs 5:18-19 NLT)

I lost my virginity during high school. It was a weekend party at a friend's house. The group that everyone wanted to be a part of was a constant in my life. A few months earlier, my acceptance into the group had been established, and I was slowly moving up the ranks. Like anything else in life, once we are accepted into an establishment, we naturally set our sights on moving up the ladder of hierarchy. The move I needed to make was "going all the way," because no one else in the group had enjoyed this ecstasy of liberation with their girlfriend.

After doing everything right for a few months, I finally convinced my girlfriend that is was the next rational step in our relationship. The excitement in her eyes of sharing the most intimate moment with someone she loved was equally matched by my thoughts of being king of the group later that night. Of course, the intoxication of finally participating in the ultimate experience with my girlfriend was exhilarating, but in the depths of my soul the intimate feelings of love were absent. Sadly, the celebration of oneness was uneventful and motivated by a sense of acceptance instead of commitment.

When a high school boy embarks on his first sexual encounter, how can it be anything but disappointing? An event that should mark the magnificence of commitment was marked by the reality of dissatisfaction. The endless hours of sexual fulfillment that we had envisioned for our first time was left to a matter of minutes of unremarkable intimacy followed by days of worrying. Using a girl that genuinely loved me to promote my own acceptance in a group of my peers was one of the lowest moments of my life, and I will forever regret it.

Broken relationships have been a struggle my entire life. It began in childhood and later materialized throughout high school and college. Relationships were more about helping me rather than bonding with another person. This led to a struggle with separation anxiety, so I slowly stopped myself from opening up to anyone about anything. In order to avoid devastating heartache, I always kept my relationships at a distance so that I would not connect with anyone. Obviously the problem with this habit is that I never experienced the beauty of a healthy relationship. Meaningful interaction with God, my wife, my child, or my parents was not achievable because I lacked a concrete relationship foundation. Whenever there is a crack in the foundation—like my warped view of relationships—then loving progression may never occur.

Hello Baptist Girls

Girls are girls, but when you meet that one who could be your wife, then everything changes. When a man changes his journey, he still carries some unwanted baggage from his previous trip, but his perspective changes. Plus it helps a little when that possible future wife is "hot!"

Some Wednesday nights while attending college, my friends and I would venture over to the large local Baptist church because we had been told about the good-looking girls in their college group. It was a typical night and we strolled in as the defiant college guys (the college and the Baptist Church had some different doctrinal views) on the prowl for girls.

Jana was a greeter that night, and she came bouncing up and introduced herself to me. She began jabbering this rehearsed speech about how great her church and college group were, and asked if we wanted more information. Two thoughts entered my mind as she rambled on. First, I wished she would shut up. She literally said more words in five minutes than I would have said in an entire day. The second thought, which had really dominated my mind, was how I would like to place my lips on that fine-looking mouth and see how far we could get in my Jeep, but she kept talking and no mouth-to-mouth contact happened that night, or in the near future. Still, she had piqued my interest enough that I agreed to work the Halloween event at their church the following weekend. I knew it would only be a matter of time before I could make my move and have a new girlfriend.

The following weekend I helped with the Halloween event and worked a booth with Jana running a carnival game for kids. I was distracted the entire time by her little honeybee outfit. I was not informed that we were supposed to wear a costume so I arrived in my regular attire, baggy sweatshirt and blue jeans. Instead of focusing on the main reason for the event that night, the kids, I was busy focusing on her cute little gymnast's body. She knew what she was doing with the kids and with me. She kept me close enough to keep me interested, but never let me cross a line that was against her beliefs (some would call it flirting).

Finally, after the event was over, I was determined to ask her out on a date. Later that week, I called her house and asked her out. She agreed but with a couple of restrictions. She said that first, her friend would come along because she did not know me. Second, she had made a decision not to kiss another guy until she had married him. I said, sure, and thought, c*hallenge accepted!*

Autumn Wedding

Jana and I met in October and got married the following October. She was the first girl I met that challenged me emotionally, spiritually, and physically. It seemed in the past that most girls were just happy to be in a relationship, but Jana was only happy if our relationship was progressing. She frequently debated with me how I could claim to be a Christian and still do the things I did everyday. She did not nag me or tell me to stop doing something, but instead engaged me in conversations asking why I was doing what I did. Many of our dates began with, *how often do you read your Bible, why don't you listen to Christian music, how can you use tobacco when you know it causes cancer, and what are your views on these doctrinal issues?* What a man will endure when he is in love with a woman.

As we began to date, Jana encouraged me to seek and be the man I pledged to be that night in Mongolia. She did not like excuses and believed people basically got what they deserved in life. I helped her understand that people make mistakes, and we needed to learn how to show compassion to them. We did not realize it then, but I believe God put us together because we both needed balance in our beliefs. This balance led us to eventually serve God overseas and minister to students in various different ways.

After a few months, the battle of "who was right" in our relationship began to fade, and a hunger for companionship began to grow. I desperately wanted to kiss her, but for the first time it was not a part of a plan for me to accomplish something. Instead, it was a yearning for our souls to encounter a profound connection, and maybe a little physical desire on my part (I am only a simple man after all). Even though I thought the basis of our relationship was growing closer to Jana, I believe it was Jana helping me grow closer to God through her. That night in Mongolia, God shared a sense of peace with me, but in returning to the States he introduced me to a beautiful woman that he knew could challenge me to a deeper relationship with him.

She was still human, though. A few months before we married, she spent the entire summer on a missions trip to Australia. In Perth, she worked at a local church and helped with a summer camp. She retuned in August and had kept a journal of the entire experience while she was there. That journal is what led to a devastating night which occurred only a few months after we were married.

One afternoon while organizing the books in our apartment, I came across her Australian journal. The temptation to read it was too overwhelming, so I started reading. I quickly learned that she had met a guy while in Australia—I'll call him "Aussie." She wrote extensively about this guy and one sentence sent me into a furious rage. "If I was not engaged to Jack, then I could see myself marrying Aussie." Are you serious? How could my own fiancée have feelings for someone else in just a few months? I had stayed in Tennessee all summer working to save money for our marriage and there she was, loving it up in Australia with some other guy.

I sat in darkness until she came home. When she walked in our apartment, I asked her one question. "Did you kiss him?" She fidgeted and said, "What are you talking about?" I threw the journal across the room and said, "This is what I am talking about." She began to cry and I started toward the door. She cried out, "I didn't kiss him, I was just writing about my honest feelings at the time." As I walked away from our apartment to the river below our campus, all I could think about was how my own wife had betrayed me after only a few months of marriage.

Jana knew where I would go and a few hours later she came down to the river to find me. It still amazes me how my wife knows me better than anyone else on this earth. As she sat down beside me, she looked into my eyes and said, "I am sorry." We began to talk and she shared how she had encountered this guy and the entire experience had swept her off her feet. She admitted that she did have some feelings for him, but she resisted any temptation to pursue those feelings. Jana apologized for hurting me and began sharing the entire story with me from beginning to end. As she continued to apologize and cry, I once again felt a peace enter my soul that I believe was a glimpse of God. Instead of focusing my anger towards her having feelings for someone else, I realized that she was genuinely committed to our marriage and me.

It is unrealistic for us to think that our spouse will never have emotional feelings or sexual desires for another person. Reality tells us this is a part of human life, and the uniqueness of a Christian marriage is the person you marry makes a commitment before God to choose you over those momentary feelings. As Jana sobbed, I took her hands and said, "I forgive you, and I love you." We entered that trial as an outraged husband and an ashamed wife, but we left that river, as a couple that understood what a marriage of commitment means to God and to each other.

Go Back and Remember

Take the time to reminisce a little bit. Talk to your wife, fiancée, or girlfriend about your first date. Think back to what it was like the first time you met and went on an official date. Talk about the fear and excitement of the event. Don't rush through the moment like we do with many other things in life. Sit and actually talk about all the magic of that moment. Think about how so many things fell in line for you to meet, go out, and eventually build a relationship together. These steps might seem foolish, but as fathers and husbands we don't want to become another statistic of a broken home. Sharing in the great moments with our significant others will help us hold fast to one another during the storms.

Tomorrow

We can decide what kind of fathers we will be for our children.

Chapter 9

What Are Fathers Teaching Their Children about Sex

But because of the temptation to sexual immorality, each man should have his own wife and each woman her own husband. The husband should give to his wife her conjugal rights, and likewise the wife to her husband. For the wife does not have authority over her own body, but the husband does. Likewise the husband does not have authority over his own body, but the wife does.
(1 Corinthians 7:2-4 ESV)

It is my opinion that people should wait until marriage to have sex.

Are you serious? Wake up, old man, this is the twenty-first century. You cannot seriously believe that a teenager in this day and society could possibly remain a virgin until finding a spouse. Why would he or she want to anyway? Having sex is one of the most exciting experiences a person will ever have in their life, and you want them to wait until something ri-

diculous like marriage. You must be a backwoods, ultra-conservative, bible-thumping preacher to even consider such a ridiculous notion.

I agree that when I consider the words, "waiting until marriage" I honestly get a sick feeling in my stomach because I immediately catch myself sounding like my old traditional parents. But like many things I have now encountered in my life, my parents might have actually had a little insight into what they were talking about when they gave me the "wait until marriage" speech. The hardest part of this ideology is the Christian component because a) our Christian teenagers are failing miserably at this biblical principle and b) non-believers are immediately going to rebel against anything viewed as a "command" from the Bible. Therefore, I will throw out any religious element of pre-marital or extra-marital sex to make my case and focus only on the intimacy of sex in its purest form. The religious aspect is vital to Christians but my approach here is to justify my argument without using biblical principles. A non-believer will not respond to a biblical principle if they have no faith in the biblical author. Likewise, many of our Christian teenagers are not mature enough to foresee the importance of the "Godly virgin principle" to stroll down the aisle on their wedding day being sexually pure. If you believe our current approach in the Christian community is effective, then Google "Christian teenagers and lost virginity statistics" in your free time.

Every year I am required to teach sexual education to my middle school physical education students. There are few things in life that I dread more than entering a room of middle school boys and discussing the subject of sex. The mere mention of words like *vagina*, *penis*, and *sexual intercourse* facilitates an explosion of giggles. If there is a purgatory, then teaching sexual education to middle school boys would definitely be included in eternal suffering.

I open every class by simply saying *penis, penis, and penis* about twenty times. The laughter and snickering finally subdues and I explain that we will not accomplish anything during the class if they insist on laughing at every word in the sexual English vocabulary. After ten minutes of going through every "offensive" word with them that I will use, I open by stating that I want to share a story with them about my own sexual experience. *There is the classroom silence I have been seeking for the past ten minutes.* As I begin this insight into my own life, I look out at sixty, sex-thirsty animals devouring every word I say in hopes of learning something that will open their eyes to a new world of sexual exploration.

Sex is one of two things for most people in this world. It is either the most intimate experience they will ever share with another person, or it is something they will perversely use to fulfill their own satisfaction. Perhaps it can be both, but in my opinion it cannot. When I first encountered sex at a young age, it was solely something to satisfy myself. Regrettably I was a selfish, immature jerk at that age and I realized sex could help me achieve something I didn't have at the time: popularity. But on my honeymoon, my wife embraced the experience as an intimate connection that she would never experience with another person. This intimacy is the element that makes sex sensational and fascinating.

Men will argue that sex is all about the climax, but most genuine men crave the intimacy of the experience in conjunction with the sexual climax. A sexual experience in which a prostitute lies on her back while faking erotic sounds will always fail in comparison to the sexual intimacy of a wife as she connects with her husband physically, emotionally, and spiritually. This is the dilemma we face as sexual beings; we hunger for the experience at a very young age, and we are willing to sacrifice the beauty of oneness for a chance to lose our virginity.

Engaging in sex with another person forms the deepest connection you could ever have with another human being. Our society continues to struggle with unwanted pregnancies, divorce, and sexually transmitted diseases because we are losing the importance of connection. We face the world's view of sex in every type of media outlet imaginable, so we are constantly being forced to embrace our sexual desires. Society tells us that spontaneous sex with numerous partners is not only acceptable, but also preferable in our enlightened culture. This false belief is a core problem with our family structure today. It has left many children in broken homes—all due to their parents' quest for temporary pleasure.

How can we ever believe that an intimate sexual experience with our spouse is erotic, when every day we are force-fed a fabrication by people we idolize that sex without boundaries is fun, carefree, and admirable? Sex without boundaries is not "fun" because most sexual experiences vastly differ from what we see in movies . It is not "carefree" unless you carry the belief that all contraceptives can prevent pregnancies and/or STDs. It is certainly not "admirable" because most people are horrified at the thought of having sex with someone that has a laundry list of previous sexual partners. Try telling your next date that you finally hit the century mark with sexual partners before her!

When men would prefer to have a one night stand in the darkness of their bedroom because they don't want to know their partner's sexual history and hide the blemishes of their own naked body from a stranger, then we have a serious problem. Is that desperate picture what we truly crave as men? For my religious friends out there, sex is not evil nor sinful. The problem is that like anything else, when sex is used outside the parameters of what it is actually intended for, it can destroy a family, a marriage, and a life in a matter of moments. Think I am being ridiculous? Talk to someone dying from an STD in the last moments of his of her life; talk to a father raising four children that lost his wife to a younger man, or talk to a teenage single mother raising a baby alone with no father.

Why does God restrict sex to marriage—to punish us? Actually, I believe God set it up this way to help us understand how wonderful sex can be when it is between two committed individuals. On our honeymoon night, I saw a passion of intimacy in the eyes of my wife that can never be described by words. She took the traditional route of cherishing the most important thing to her marriage and waited until our honeymoon night to have sex. On that night, Jana gave me every part of her mind, body, and soul in a loving commitment for the reminder of our lives. That hot summer night many years earlier when I foolishly threw away my virginity robbed me of experiencing the same profound connection with my wife on that sacred evening. The intimate connection of oneness with our future spouse is what we are missing out on when we become sexually active early in life.

Why should we teach our children to wait? Sexual intimacy is the combining of two fleshes into one; nothing else can ever achieve this connection between two people. We have taken sex and turned it into a fast food climatic experience with another person. When your child makes the decision to give away his or her virginity, shouldn't it be with someone who has committed before God, friends, and family to be their lifelong partner? Do we really want our children to be on sexual conquests before marraige?

Most people in this world view having sex only after exchanging marriage vows as outdated and traditional. Somehow, our world has become a place where conceding to our sexual desires before marriage is viewed as a necessary accomplishment before becoming a "mature adult." Instead, we should encourage our children to preserve sex for the one person whom they plan to embrace every morning for the remainder of their lives.

Let me close by sharing what I have observed teaching high school students over the past fifteen years. Kids want to be accepted and loved. Just like the rest of us, they desire for someone to view them as significant. If that means a young girl must give herself to a boy on a conquest, then she will. If that means a boy must view girls as sexual goals, then he will. Sex is just an avenue our children use when trying to find love and acceptance. Teaching our children the importance of sex requires us to embrace the reason our children feel unloved and unaccepted. You can help your children choose how to live their sexual lives.

Having premarital sex damaged my marriage in ways that can never be repaired. Regardless of forgiveness or reconciliation, there will always be something missing because I did not wait for Jana. I challenge you to really think through this idea of sex before marriage and make your own decision about what you will teach your children.

Make Amends

This next challenge is going to sound ridiculous but hear me out. If you lost your virginity before marriage, then I encourage you to write a letter to the person of that first sexual encounter. It should be even easier with social media.

I did this many years ago and apologized to that person for how things ended. Before writing the letter, I talked to Jana about it first. Then I was able to find out the contact information of the person I wrote the letter to. I did not agree to meet her in person, but instead sent her my letter so I could keep a safe distance and she could think about it before responding back. It brought a sense of reconciliation into my life. The letter was not dramatic or extremely long, I simply confessed the broken promises.

Maybe your first sexual experience was different or maybe you are unable to contact that person. Regardless, at least for me, bringing some closure and forgiveness to that experience healed a burden I had carried for many years.

This reconciliation can empower you to take the next step to talk with your children about sex. You and your wife should sit down with them when he or she reaches an appropriate age and talk about it in an open and honest way. Don't put it off until they are twenty years old. Frivolous sex is destroying our children's lives. No one is better prepared to talk to your children about this than you and your spouse. Help them understand sex, and, if needed, give them the opportunity to heal from previous sexual experiences. Being a father requires us to accept being uncomfortable sometimes for the benefit of our children.

Chapter 10

Fathers, Let's Embrace This Final Question of God

Not everyone who says to me, "Lord, Lord," will enter the kingdom of heaven, but only he who does the will of my Father who is in heaven. (Matthew 7:21 NIV)

So let's see. In the past few chapters we have journeyed from God, to marriage, to sex, and now back to God. I am pretty sure this is not the traditional transition we take when talking about Christian doctrine. But by now, you know that I don't always follow conventional thought processes when discussing beliefs. One month before writing this book, I talked to a couple in Taiwan who had just given birth to a son with Down syndrome. I shared many of my experiences raising Marley, as well as some struggles I was experiencing. During the conversation, I stopped myself and said, "Actually, I would certainly be classified as mentally unstable, so talking to me about Down syndrome might not be the best course of action for your family." They started laughing and the wife made the comment, "Who is really stable in this world?"

Sharing honest chapters with you is how I have been able to transition back to the issue of God's existence after exploring sex and relationships. One fundamental flaw I see in our existence as human beings is the belief that these issues are not uniquely connected. For years, we have tried to separate these issues into independent matters. Topics of God's existence, approaches to sexual experiences, and family roles are usually studied individually, and not as a collective group. The reason for this approach is because we believe that including personal beliefs into anything we teach is absurd. God, family, and sex are the foundation of who we are and what we will become in life. Which three other topics are more essential in understanding our own lives or the lives of our children? In my opinion, these issues are woven together in the same nature as a beautiful tapestry. When you leave out an essential thread in a tapestry, you will never have a complete masterpiece. How can we fully understand God, family, or sex without knowledge of the other two?

When I teach sex education in school, I inject questions about religious beliefs and family models. When I discuss the existence of God, I connect family structure and sexual temptation. If we look at the different dynamics of a family, then we explore religious teachings about family structures and sexual experiences in relation to the family; they are all interconnected. Attempting to separate these issues into disparate categories leads us to teaching nothing substantial. Figuring out our belief systems regarding God, sex, and family are the cornerstones of our lives. How can I jump so casually through these essential sections? Because if you are not willing to openly study the significance of how these major events interact with one another, then you will always be treating the symptoms and not healing the person.

Is there a God? If you are still haunted by that question then I challenge you to search your soul and find the answer. Regardless of your stance on religion, I know that your belief or non-belief in God will affect how you live your life and the decisions you make for yourself and your family. This acceptance of God has been a lifelong process for me and was greatly challenged when my daughter was born. There are days when I can feel God in the room beside me, and days when I feel like God is non-existent. The entire process is a battle, but the outcome is essential for our lives and eternity. Unfortunately, most people are frightened to truthfully confront this question, so they fill their lives with clutter. They remain busy with various activities like employment, relationships, sports, media, and various other things until death darkens their door. Then when death forces a, "Is there a God?" moment, people procrastinate by stating that these questions must be answered before even considering the possibility of God. *How can there be a God with so much suffering in this world? How can a God let these things happen to me?*

I want to share my opinion on the most frequent question I get when facing the question of God's existence. *If there is a God then how can we have suffering in this world?* This is a question that I wrestled with for months after my daughter was born with Down syndrome. Several people would tell me that Jana and I were chosen as special parents for Marley, and she was made exactly in God's image, but people are made in God's image, not disabilities. Down syndrome is not a blessing from God, but instead a genetic abnormality. Children are born with Down syndrome just like children are born blind, deaf, or autistic. Don't stand there with your "normal" children and tell me I should feel blessed because God gave me a child with Down syndrome. I do not believe God gave Marley Down syndrome, but I believe he can bring good out of it.

That is the difference when looking at the existence of God. We want to blame our suffering on God, but the problem is suffering comes from choice. We cannot take away suffering without taking away free will. No murders, then no free will to kill others; no adultery, then no free will to have sex outside of marriage; no weather catastrophes, then no free will to do things that will alter the environment. Marley was born with Down syndrome because we live in a fallen world. Terrible things occur every day in this life and that is a result of us living a life on this earth. If you truly wanted to remove all the suffering from this life, then you must accept no free will in this life.

These two things are interconnected. Free will embodies evil, which leads to human suffering. Every day we choose how we use our free will, and whether or not it invokes good or evil. God is active in this world and he intervenes. However, we must understand that if he always intercedes to eliminate suffering, then that would also sacrifice our human free will.

Marley was born with a genetic disorder and the cause of that extra chromosome has not been discovered. God's plan did not involve punishing her or us with a genetic disorder because I now believe in a God of love. Babies are born every day with disorders that are likely linked to nutrition, chemicals, disease exposure, and numerous other factors that have not been discovered. Our lack of discovery cannot automatically lead us to blaming God. And when we do make medical advances, then maybe we are catching glimpses of a divine Creator instead of disproving him.

When Marley was born, I entered into a deep depression in which I blamed God for her condition. Actually, God did not cause the condition, but rather he used her differences to teach me things that I would have never learned without her. Maybe non-believers see it as a curse on my family, but I have encountered a deeper understanding of love, compassion, and acceptance because Marley entered my life. The glory of God can be magnified when we accept the suffering and realize that God wants to embrace us during our times of sorrow.

This is the only chapter in this book that I will not close with a challenge. The reason for this variation is because this chapter requires more from you that just a few moments or a simple letter. The answer to this question will be the basis of your life. Whether you believe it or not, the decisions and choices you make are going to be greatly influenced by your belief or lack of belief in God.

Early in this book I encouraged you to only consider the question of God's existence. Now I ask you to dedicate some time to finding the answer. Regardless, you will never be completely at peace with your decision, and there will always be moments when you question the existence of God. I believe this is a natural progression that deepens our relationship with our Creator. I find myself truly seeking God when I can find no hope in this world. No one can force you to believe in God but you need to at least take the time to search for the answer. Even when I question God and openly rebuke him, I can still sense his presence. There is something different about life when you believe God's purpose is present in your daily routine.

Non-believers will state that belief in God is just a safety net people need to survive. I agree that we all need God to survive. Writing this book would not be possible without a belief in God. On the days I want to give up and move on, my belief—no matter how weak it is—pushes me forward. I believe there is a heaven and I believe God has a purpose for my daughter, my family, and me.

Dedicate some time to looking at this life-changing issue—we owe it to ourselves and to our children to search for an answer to this question. Christians always tell us we are missing out on something in life if we don't believe in God. If they were somehow right, wouldn't you want to spend a little time to see what it was? Maybe in the end you will find that there is nothing to be missed. But maybe, you will find a Creator that wants to build a relationship and navigate with you through this journey of life.

If you take that final step and decide to believe in God, then that is not the conclusion of your journey. Christianity calls us to a relationship with God through his son Jesus Christ. Our hope is not in a distant figure that we idolize, but in an intimate connection with the being that created the world. Christian faith is rooted in a daily walk with God. Like any relationship, there will be hurdles and triumphs but that is the uniqueness of faith. The Christian belief opens a door to a spiritual exchange that you can experience in everyday life. The hardest concept for me to grasp about God is that he cares about *my* mundane life. He desires to be a part of *your* life every day of the week—and not just Sundays. This is where many believers "miss the boat" with their beliefs. We see God as someone distant who we cannot understand or connect with on a personal level. We go through the motions every Sunday, but that sincere personal bond is nonexistent. If you choose to take that final step of acceptance, then don't fall into the ordinary trap that devours many Christians. Be determined to spend time with God. Personally, I fail at this routinely, but it is a necessity to embrace the true character of God. A good first step, which I often reference, is audibly talking to God. Force yourself to talk to God and spend some time in the scriptures. If you make this a daily habit, then you will force yourself to draw closer to him. It would be impossible for me to spend every day with another person and not learn about their nature and uniqueness. Take the same approach with your beliefs and build a relationship with the being that breathed the breath of life into your lungs.

Chapter 11

Pursuing Perfection Cannot Dictate How We View Others

Do not judge so that you will not be judged. For in the way you judge, you will be judged; and by your standard of measure, it will be measured to you. Why do you look at the speck that is in your brother's eye, but do not notice the log that is in your own eye? Or how can you say to your brother, "Let me take the speck out of your eye," and behold, the log is in your own eye? You hypocrite, first take the log out of your own eye, and then you will see clearly to take the speck out of your brother's eye. (Matthew 7:1-5 NASB)

It started as a harmless joke—something we did regularly among my group of friends in middle school. We were notorious for pulling off extreme pranks and this girl looked like the perfect target. I was new to the group, and I knew this one venture could solidify my belonging. She was a little different from the rest of us and she only attended PE class anyway. If we had a little fun at her expense then who would really care? Plus she struggled to communicate so we could avoid any discipline from the principal. The point was to have a little fun teasing this girl and move on with life. We were bored, and welcomed any mischief to brighten up a hum-drum school day.

Word got out that she had a crush on me. At first it was embarrassing, but like any typical middle school bully, I quickly saw an opportunity for humiliation. My buddies were all in on it, and they agreed to go along with the prank. She was overweight and had a learning disability, but sympathy did not register at the time. The only thing I saw was an outcast girl who was only around us during one class and break time. The plan was launched during lunch, and I gave my friend a note to pass along to her. It was a simple note that everyone was familiar with in those formative years. The note said, "Will you be my girlfriend? Yes, No, or Maybe / Love Jack."

It was perfect. We all knew she liked me because she had made it very public and open to everyone at our school. The note solidified the ridiculous feelings she had for me and was returned within the hour. How could she really think I would be interested in being her boyfriend? She was a disabled girl who no one liked, and I was one of the most popular boys in school! She took the bait, hook, line, and sinker. Before I knew it, we were hanging out together at lunchtime, break time, and during class. Behind her back, everyone giggled and taunted this farce of a relationship we claimed to have. She never realized that this was an enormous prank and she was the unknowing victim. The charade carried on for a few weeks until like anything else, we became bored with the entire adventure. Finally one day after PE class, I broke the news to her. The tragedy of the moment was lost to my immature mind, but I witnessed the devastating effect it had on her. I simply told her I wanted to break up because I was bored. She immediately broke down and started sobbing uncontrollably. The entire situation was awkward for me because my friends were watching, so I just walked away while this poor girl cried with anguish. For the remainder of the year, she avoided my friends and I at gym class and lunchtime. For us, it was just another well-executed gag, but regrettably, I knew it was not just a joke to her.

Life in my family's house was about achieving perfection. If you set your mind to accomplish something and you are determined to achieve that goal, then you will find success. This was the basis for everything we did at my house. My father would often tell me to not do something "half -***". Basically that meant that when you tackled a chore like cleaning the garage, you moved everything in the garage in order to clean behind it! In my childhood home, there were no short cuts. If you could not do something correctly, then you didn't do it at all. This was a great motto for me to live by as a teenager and even now as an adult, but it warped one view I had in my life: the view I had of people with disabilities.

Perfection is what we all strive for in life, one way or another. Even now, I try to do things perfectly. I don't want someone to look at me and think, "What a failure." When I look back at the tragic day that I decided to deceive this girl, I question why I ever thought it would be funny to mock her. In my opinion, it came down to naively thinking she was a lesser person than me. Why did I indulge that horrible thought? Because I concluded that her disabilities made her an incomplete person and that she was not equal to my friends and me. This inner drive to be perfect and accepted would never happen for her, so she was insignificant in my eyes. I was pushed to succeed and the only thing that could limit me was my own laziness. When I looked at someone with a handicap, I equated their disability with a lifetime of personal failure. This difference dominated my thoughts, so the thought of this classmate being a person like me was unacceptable. Sure I could have had sympathy and coddled her, but in no way could anyone expect me to approach her like my "normal friends." Society, education, parenting, and peers could all be blamed for my horrendous view of my classmate, but eventually I had to examine my own heart and beliefs. Like many people I now meet, I carried this superiority mentality that she was not my equivalent. I was like everyone else and she was not. Unfortunately I believed this lie and it instantly separated me from her. Viewing her as just another classmate was impossible because my own warped mind believed that somehow I was more important to society that she was.

Some people say that God will force us to "own up" to our past sins. I am not sure that concept applies to my situation, but it is something I have thought about now that my daughter is the disabled girl in the class. Karma is another religious belief here in Thailand, and I am sure several people would use that description to explain my journey from a bullying middle school student to a desperate father. Regardless, this is the new journey I face with my family, and now looking back at that incident in middle school, I am sickened by it. Did that girl go home and tell her family what happened that day at school? If she did, then why did they never complain to the school? Did she keep it a secret and quietly suffer alone from our bullying? Did my hurtful prank alter her entire outlook on life? I will never know the answer to those questions, and to this day, there are times when I wonder whether the negative outcomes of her life are a result of my one regretful prank.

Regardless of karma, God, or fate, I now stand to the side and observe *my* daughter being left out during playtime. Already at the age of three, I see that the other children usually prefer to play with kids like themselves instead of with Marley. Sure, our community of Christian families encourage their children to play with Marley, but there are just certain milestones that she has not accomplished that set her apart from the others. As the other children run and jabber, she tries to walk extremely fast and communicate with her limited vocabulary. How can you blame a child for not wanting to hang out with someone that is on a different level developmentally? But the problem of treating the disabled differently doesn't just stop at childhood, it runs through the course of society's lives, regardless of age.

I remember a time Marley suddenly got sick in the middle of the night. She was running a temperature of 102°F so we took her to the emergency room. We were led to the ER where we saw a doctor who was unfamiliar to us. Marley was snuggled up against Jana's chest because it was obvious that she felt terrible. While the doctor talked to us about Marley's symptoms, she finally asked Jana to turn Marley around in order to examine her ears and throat. At that moment Marley's little head popped up from Jana's chest and she looked at the doctor. Suddenly the doctor shrieked and said, "Does your daughter have a disease?" At first I was confused and I just looked over at Jana. Does Marley have a disease? I thought, "What is she talking about? That is why we came to the hospital; because we are worried she has caught something." Then it suddenly clicked in my mind. She was talking about Marley having Down syndrome. I quickly stated that Marley had Down syndrome and held Jana's hand. Jana was on the verge of delivering a tongue-lashing that would not only be painful for this doctor but also not beneficial for our sick daughter. Cutting Jana off, I steered the conversation towards why Marley was feeling sick. After a few tense moments, Jana's face returned to a regular color, and Marley was diagnosed with a bacterial infection.

That night after putting Marley to bed, I thought about what the doctor had said about Marley having a disease. Does she have a disease? The reaction on the doctor's face was the look of *what is wrong with your daughter?* It reminded me of looking at someone in a horror movie who was severely disfigured. That night was just another reminder that my daughter was different and that for the remainder of her life, this is how the world would view her regardless of her accomplishments.

So what do we do? How can we change a perception we have about a person when that perception has dominated our thoughts since birth? It is not an easy thing to do. My own daughter has a disability, and yet I still feel uncomfortable around other people with disabilities.

Earlier in the book, I had told you that my dad used to drive around a severely-handicapped man in our community. Today, this man still wanders the streets of my hometown trying to function in a society that has forgotten about him. I never understood why my father was so kind and generous to this man who was not able to return the favors. My father once told me that when they were growing up, this man had no learning disability or psychological problem. I asked my dad how this man ended up with no family or friends to take care of him. My father informed me that the wandering man in our town had been beaten his entire childhood by his alcoholic father. It got so bad at one point that he was taken to the hospital for his injuries. The injuries left permanent brain damage and his condition continued to deteriorate throughout his life.

My father had compassion for this man because he was a childhood friend. It was more than just pity, it was a genuine relationship. That is the difference for us as we embrace people not exactly like us in society. The issue is not whether to assist disabled people or have sympathy for them. The answer to fixing our delusion is by taking the time to get to know people who are disabled. Try to build a real relationship with someone who the world sees as different.

My daughter has Down syndrome and I have accepted that for her life and for mine. But when I look at her, I see Marley, not a girl with Down syndrome. The only reason I embrace this view is because I now have a human bond with her. Without this meaningful bond, she would just be another handicapped girl who I would console because of her condition. People with disabilities do not want empathy or handouts. These people, like us, bring something unique and vibrant to our society. They desire what we desire—friendships. Sure it is not always easy, but it is not always easy being friends with the so-called "regular people" in life either. The next time you encounter someone in your circle who is a little different than you, consider taking the time to befriend that person. It might change your life in a way that you could have never imagined.

Step Outside the Box

I think this challenge might be difficult for you because it was for me. Take the time and put yourself and your family in a group of people with whom you are uncomfortable being around. I routinely force myself to spend time with disabled people. I do this because the more I am around someone with a disability, the more comfortable I feel. This level of peace enables me to confront my fears and build a relationship with that person. Try to find an organization in your area where your family could spend time developing new friendships. Don't go into this trying to help or serve someone else, but instead, go into this venture determined to cast off your preconceived beliefs about disabled people, and make some genuine friends. You and your family might be amazed by what you will find, and might even be surprised by how much you actually have in common with someone who you thought was so different from you.

Chapter 12

Save Your Marriage and Raise Your Children

Husbands, love your wives, just as Christ loved the church and gave himself up for her. (Ephesians 5:25 NIV)

There is an epidemic right now in the Christian church. It is something rarely talked about and has not been adequately addressed in our congregations. In fact, I believe some people view it as a necessary evil in the call of raising children. Almost like a sacrifice that needs to be made in keeping a marriage together until a child leaves home. The epidemic I am referring to is the practice of Christian couples seeking a divorce as soon as their children leave for college or move out.

The reason I specifically refer to Christian couples is because I think that they are directly responsible for this problem throughout society. As Christians, we are called to live a life that represents Christ. This commandment often persuades couples to remain in a loveless marriage for the sake of their children. For some reason, these couples believe that staying with their spouse for the sake of the children is *their* cross to bear. The problem is marriage was not intended to be a system that we hold together in order to just raise our children. If the world sees empty nest divorce being accepted in our Christian culture, then that opens the door to the criticism, "Even Christians can't make a marriage work after their children leave home." In fact, this line of thinking, *hold it together for the kids*, could be referenced as an argument supporting this book. **Failing at Fatherhood** is a book based on sacrificing for our children. Does that mean we should stay committed in a loveless marriage for our children? God calls us to commit to our wife first, then consider the possibility of children. Divorce is not the answer, but neither is living a lie in a loveless marriage. We can choose to have both—children in a loving marriage—if we are diligent in being committed spiritual fathers to our children and husbands to our wives. A healthy husband is determined to overcome obstacles to continually love his wife everyday. A healthy father is committed to staying in the home and raising his children in a Godly manner. These two words, *father* and *husband*, are separated in the English language, but as committed men, we must learn to fulfill both these roles interchangeably and treat the words as if it were one.

Let's look at this statistic from the National Center For Family and Marriage:

> Statistic for people who divorce after age 50 - The divorce rate for this group doubled between 1990 and 2010, according to a study by the National Center for Family and Marriage Research at Bowling Green State University in Ohio. "This surprised us, because the rate

> for younger people has leveled off," said lead researcher Susan Brown, a sociology professor. "In 1990, only 1 in 10 divorces were people 50 and older. Now it's 1 in 4."

How do we continue a marriage of love and intimacy? First, we must not use our children as an escape from dealing with our marital problems. I know a couple that was married for thirty-plus years with two children. The day the last child left for college, the truth came out. One spouse had been involved in an extramarital affair for several years before sharing the truth about the relationship. The children, according to the spouse, were the only things that kept the marriage functional for the last two years. The marriage was just a front to help the family stay together for the sake of the children. What are we teaching our sons and daughters when we abruptly end our marriage as soon as they leave home? Maybe you are saying, "Well at least they stayed together till the children left." To a degree that is true, and at least compared to the numerous fathers that have left before or immediately after a child is born, it counts for something. However, the problem here is that our kids know the truth whether we as parents admit it or not.

There is a specific date in history that every couple commits to one another in front of God and family to stay together. That commitment was not until children entered adulthood, it was "'till death." How can one be a productive father and not a serving husband to one's wife? You can't—and your children see your true nature as husbands and wives on a daily basis. We can't conceal when our marriage has lost its commitment and intimacy from our children. Kids are not given enough credit for what they learn and observe from their parents. Ninety percent of what I do now as a parent is from having observed my own parents. Even the things I hope to change about my own parenting techniques are due to how my parents raised me. Our children are a significant attribute to our family, but they are not the center of our family. We must remember that our wives came before our kids. The day we walked down the aisle was a promise to them—before we ever thought about making a promise to our children.

When I was in college, I had a professor that talked about an elderly couple in a church he led before becoming a professor. He explained that it became well known in the church congregation that this couple had a "sex day." Every Sunday afternoon this couple dedicated to lovemaking. Family, friends, and other acquaintances knew not to visit their home on Sunday afternoons because of the activities in the bedroom. I remember sitting in his class and thinking that the notion of having a sex day was ridiculous. Of course, at that time, I was not ten-plus years into a marriage with my wife. Make having sex with your spouse a priority in your marriage.

Some marriages don't struggle with sexual intimacy but there are other couples who do. We all become overwhelmed with work, finances, raising children, and numerous other tasks that interfere with our sex life. At first it may not be a huge problem to go a week or two without being sexually active, but this routine can lead to disharmony in a marriage. We are created to be sexual beings. When intimacy, which I believe is the central driving force of a marriage, is not present, then that marriage is going to suffer. The divorced couple I referenced earlier in this chapter went over two years without being sexually active before the affair. We cannot abstain from sex and maintain a healthy marriage. If you believe a lack of sex is interfering with the health of your marriage, then consider implementing a sex day. Set a certain time aside every week that you are going to be intimate with your wife. Perhaps decide to use a sex day like a safety net in your marriage. If you get to that day in the week without being sexually active, then make a commitment to have sex on that day. It amazes me how well Jana and I get along when our sex life is healthy and vibrant.

Finally, pray and worship together. This is still something that Jana and I struggle with—even after thirteen years of marriage. The reason I make this suggestion is because it has a dual benefit for your marriage. The first obvious benefit is the relationship you and your spouse will develop with God. We are taught as Christians that when you marry, you become one flesh. This one flesh has the ability to accomplish great things for the kingdom that one could never have done alone. Worshipping, praying, and studying the scriptures together will not only strengthen your relationship with God, but will also enhance your marriage.

The other benefit that I am referring to is "couple openness." This is the most critical element of spending time together with God. When Jana and I pray together, we talk. When Jana and I do devotions together, we talk. And when Jana and I worship our Lord together, we talk. The biggest obstacle to overcome in any marriage is communication. Let's be honest; men are terrible at communicating and being open with anyone, even with our wives. Our wife should not only be our life-long companion, but also our best friend. I learned very early in my marriage that if I could not share my inner thoughts and fears with my wife, then being a successful husband would not be possible. Of course, this is not always easy.

For a time in our marriage I was struggling with some sexual issues. It was a very difficult time for me and after much turmoil; I finally confessed it to Jana. The response from her was not what I expected. She admitted to having some of the same struggles, and we were able to embrace our failures together. Do I share everything with Jana? No, because I still struggle in this area of my life. But I am slowly learning that the more honest and open I am with the woman I call my wife, the stronger our marriage becomes. We must learn to talk, share, and confess to one another to reinforce our marriage and relationship with God. Marriage is a journey of love and commitment. I once heard marriage described as *the* only commitment we must continually work at to keep alive. This is only partially true. I don't want to spend the remainder of my life just working to "save" my marriage. Our marriages need to be based on honesty, intimacy, and God. If we can do these three things, then we will see our love grow, and our marriage will become something our children will admire and aspire to for their own lives. Marriage cannot be a constant battle. Marriage needs to be a constant journey in which we discover new things everyday with our spouse. This will lead to a deeper connection that exceeds anything we envisioned the day we stood before God exchanging vows.

Make a List

This is going to be very simple. Sit down with your wife and make a list of non-negotiable items for your marriage. To start, make a list of three items that you are going to implement in your marriage over the next year. If you are really brave then put the list on your refrigerator, or where it will be seen every day to be a reminder to you and your wife. An example list would look like this:

- *Pray every night together before going to bed*
- *Have a date night once every two weeks*
- *Make Sunday afternoon sexy time if it has not happened that week*

You need to decide which things you want to include in your list. These things will make your marriage stronger. Communication is the key to a healthy marriage and the sooner we realize this as husbands the better men we will be. Maybe find another couple to join with you in making a list. This will allow you to be accountable to one another. Jana and I have started to implement some routines in our marriage and it has greatly helped us communicate more with one another and God.

CHAPTER 13

Embrace the Future without Worrying About It

So don't worry about tomorrow, for tomorrow will bring its own worries. Today's trouble is enough for today. (Matthew 6:34 NLT)

As we come towards the end of the book, I want to assure you that I have very little figured out in life. This book is intended to tell my story and share my take-aways from my own journey which may prompt other fathers to take action. It is certainly not a final solution to solve the disarray in our lives. I struggle daily with numerous things and the most prominent one is the future of my daughter. I constantly find myself contemplating the "what ifs" in life. The worries of tomorrow can dominate our daily thoughts and lead us down a path of destruction and loss. Recently, I came across a great exchange from the comic strip, Peanuts.

Violet: What are you two standing here looking so worried about?

Charlie Brown: We're afraid of the future!

Violet: Are you worried about anything in particular?

Charlie Brown: Oh, no. We're worried about everything!

Linus: Yes, our worrying is very broadminded!

One time Marley got a rash that we suspected were from mosquitoes because of the numerous red bites. Most Saturday mornings we go to school and Marley plays on the playground with the other children. She loves this time and it is great for her development. She runs, pushes, and climbs with all the other kids. That afternoon, we got home and noticed she had numerous bites on her legs and arms. Since we live in a tropical country, mosquitoes are a constant pest that we battle on a daily basis. We did not think much about the bites until a few days later when the red bumps started to develop puss pockets. This led me to an immediate alert level and I dove head first into researching this on the Internet. I started searching about rashes and was desperately trying to find an answer for my daughter's mysterious bumps. We were debating taking her to the doctor but the bites did not seem to be bothering her. Some rashes seemed to fit my Google search and some did not. With my limited medical experience, I could not figure out which rash she had on her body so I started to broaden my search. The panic started to set in when I read that rashes could sometimes be a sign of leukemia. Suddenly my mind jumped down a path of fear and worry. I went from a simple rash, to leukemia, to incurable, to moving back to the States, and to finally my daughter dying. This illogical thought process transpired in a matter of seconds and I had already accepted this as the fate of my daughter. How quickly our minds can be overcome by irrational thoughts when we travel down an unreasonable road of insanity!

The next morning Jana took Marley in to see the doctor, not because of my panic, but because we already had a scheduled check-up appointment for Marley that day. It turned out that she had been bitten by mites while playing in the grass. The doctor gave us a steroid cream to apply to the rash, and it disappeared within a few days.

One obstacle we must overcome as parents is the fear of something tragic happening to our child. With today's media, we become overwhelmed by tragedies that happen to families on a daily basis. This bombardment of what can go wrong can dominate our daily lives. So how can we handle this anxiety? This is not an easy question to answer because once again it goes back to what you believe.

Recently I heard a preacher speaking about dealing with a fear of the future. He stated that our responsibility is obedience to God, and God's responsibility is the outcome. Basically we are called to follow God, and whatever happens in our lives is God's responsibility. This is not an easy teaching to follow especially if you are not a follower of God. Christians are raised to have faith in God directing our future. What that means is simply that the future is in God's hands, and we have to trust him in guiding us through it.

We have been discussing the idea of faith and trust throughout the book. The complication that comes with this thinking is actually allowing someone else to be in control. It reminds me of an old Bob Dylan song that states, we got to serve somebody: “Well it may be the devil or it may be the Lord, but you’re gonna have to serve somebody.” There is a lot of truth in that statement and most of us hate being accountable to anything or anyone. But there is a sliver of hope that I have found in this idea of trusting God with the future. The problem is that we are not guaranteed an easy future in scripture. In fact, God warns us that our future might involve suffering and pain and that we should even expect it. The same can be said for non-believers in regards to their future plans. Nothing is guaranteed and we will all experience hardships in life.

The sliver of hope I mentioned earlier, when thinking about my daughter’s future, is the idea that God loves Marley more than I love her. That, in itself is powerful. I know today, as I write this sentence, that other than Jana, I love my daughter more than anyone else in the world. I have shared with you a time when I struggled loving my daughter, but I have come to develop an immense love for her. Therefore, I care about what happens to her, I think about ways that I can help her in life, and I do everything I can to support her. According to the Christian faith, however, God loves her even more than I do. Imagine a God that actually weeps when Marley suffers. When she is sick, or something tragic happens to her, God actually hurts with her. Could God love her so much that he would give anything for her including his own life? That is what we are taught from an early age in reference to Christ dying on the cross. If this idea that “God loves Marley beyond my understanding” is true, then why should I worry about her future? Even if the worst happens, if the Christian faith is true, then she will spend an eternity with her Creator. If you can accept that God loves your child more than you do, then any fear of the future should be thwarted because the Creator of the universe is watching over your child.

What if you don't believe in God? Again it is time to figure out your stance on a Creator. I believe that all these things are interconnected and you have to start at a foundational belief in God. There is a direct separation that comes between believers and non-believers with regards to this issue. The division comes in death, because Christians see victory whereas non-Christians do not. If my daughter died today, then I would be reunited with her in eternity. That is the hope we carry through death. Unfortunately, that optimism is vacant when faith is not present. Maybe eternal life is legitimate or maybe not, but nevertheless, this division cannot be dismissed between believers and non-believers.

The problem with this entire book is the notion of trying to connect with believers and non-believers. There comes a point where you must choose a side and when you do your views and opinions will change. But, maybe you say it is a false hope to believe in life after death, and maybe you are right, but it is still a doctrine that cannot be ignored when worrying about the future.

Yet, regardless of your belief or lack of belief, what does worrying accomplish? My wife would always ask me, "What are you gaining when you worry about Marley's future?" This is true because no matter how much we worry, it is not going to alter our future. The things that are going to happen are going to happen no matter how much we worry about them. As humans, we always look for some kind of defense against future evil, and for some reason, the act of worrying becomes our weapon of choice. "I can't do anything to help the situation but, if I worry enough about it, then that might help my cause." Of course, this is a ridiculous notion, but when nothing else works, we grasp for any hope that we believe can make a difference. Mournfully, this is all I can really offer to those with no belief in God. I have spent a substantial amount of time thinking of ways to help non-believers overcome fear, but at the end of the day, I cannot. Perhaps as you are reading this, you are thinking of ways you can overcome fear without God being present in your life (I can see you saying, "Ha, I don't need God because I use this technique and handle fear just fine.") Maybe you have stress figured out and my belief in a God is just a sad crutch that I use to deal with my uncertain future. Regardless, I am starting to find peace in the security of God loving my daughter. I can't dismiss all the anxieties in my life, but when those anxious moments come, I find myself repeating a phrase I heard from that preacher a few months ago, "The outcome is in God's hands."

As we wrap up this chapter, I want to encourage you in one other avenue of dealing with anxiety and fear. If you need help outside of your own family, then go out and get it. We often approach things like anxiety with a fearless belief that we can overcome it all by ourselves. We, men especially, carry this superior toughness that anything in this life can be defeated without help from others. When one of our fellow men gets outside help to deal with something, we sometimes see them as weak. *Was he not tough enough to deal with it himself?* One comment that still sticks out to this day from my CNN article was from one of these ultra macho men. He stated that if he had as much estrogen as me, according to the way I wrote the article, then he would suggest my wife leave me because I was a wimp. That one hurt.

When someone questions your manhood, then the first response is to man up. Even as I write about this, I want to tell you how much I bench press, how awesome I am in the bedroom, and how many animals I have killed in my life. That is the nature of us as men, but that aspect of our mind often crushes the emotional make-up of our soul. If you need help with anything in your life, then shame cannot prevent you from finding that help. Does that make you less of a man? Does opening up your soul and saying something is wrong make you less of a husband? Wouldn't it be better to address these issues instead of continuing to damage your marriage, family, and your own life? Finding counselors and therapists to help you deal with your fears is a noble act that should be encouraged.

I watched a video by a man who talks about living in a "man box." It was a great video presentation about how we have taken "being a man" and turned it into something barbaric that suppresses women. We have to move past this idea that men should not share their emotions or fears. Sharing with our family about our internal struggles is *essential* to our call as fathers. You can both cry, and still be tough at the same time. You can seek help and still "be manly." You can believe in God and worship him without being weak. If you are struggling, then ignore the traditional mindset of toughing it out alone. Get the support that you need to save your marriage, family, and self.

Confront Your Fears

This may sound trivial, but it is something I remember doing one time at a retreat that was very beneficial to me. Take a moment and write down the top five fears you currently have in your life. After you write them down, take about five minutes to meditate on those fears. As you meditate, think about why you fear these things. What circumstances in your life are making these items a constant fear for you? If you believe in God then audibly give these fears over to him. State out loud that you want God to take hold of these fears and give you peace from worrying about them. Once you finish, light the piece of paper on fire. Make sure the fire is controlled and watch your worries burn to ashes. Take that moment to free yourself from worrying about those five concerns you just scorched. Finally, when those desperate moments return in the future and you find yourself worrying about these possibilities, take a minute and repeat, "It is in God's hands." He is responsible for the outcome, not you.

Marley

You have changed my life, but I have failed you as a father.

Chapter 14

Marley's Love for Her Father

I tell you the truth, unless you change and become like little children, you will never enter the kingdom of heaven. (Matthew 18:3 NIV)

One of my good friends, who is now a missionary in Papua New Guinea, told me before Marley was born that babies were fairly boring the first year of their lives. He commented that they do the same things around the clock: cry, eat, and sleep. This held true for Marley the first year of her life. While I was struggling with a deep depression, Jana was busy caring for Marley's every need. . Marley's interaction with me was very limited, but Jana had been able to build a special connection by caring for Marley. I quickly became jealous of Jana and furious that the healing process I was desperately seeking, could not be accomplished with my own daughter. This led me to looking for reconciliation outside of my house by talking with other families.

The animosity that was building daily with my family was

hindering my ability to heal. I desperately wanted to find a way to emerge from the evil pit of depression, but my family was busy being a family. Jana did not have time to care for a failing husband and a newborn baby. Marley was too busy doing her three daily duties to really connect with an unapproachable father. I turned to the Internet to find answers, and began researching Down syndrome every moment I had free. The research led me to a group entitled "Einstein syndrome," and through this group, I quickly became connected with a unique Down syndrome community in the USA. Bangkok is twelve hours ahead of the East Coast, so this led to an interesting start to each morning at work. For several months, I would begin each day by calling a family in the States that had a child with Down syndrome. These families helped me discover other families throughout the world that were embracing a new life with Down syndrome.

I called a man in India that had a son with Down syndrome, and we talked for hours about our families and futures. The honest conversations we shared led to a friendship I would have never encountered without Marley. Even though our cultures and faiths were completely different, we shared the one common thing that had become the mainstay in our lives, our child's condition.

These families took precious time out of their hectic lives to talk to me about my family and daughter. I created an amazing support group for myself and would rotate through different people every two weeks. I had about fifteen different "counselors" who I would talk with and each one offered valuable insight because they were living the same life-changing situation. These families shared openly and honestly about their experiences, and what I could expect from society. They helped me travel a journey of acceptance and anticipation of being a father for Marley. These fantastic families took precious time from their own busy lives and helped me survive a Down syndrome diagnosis and ultimately reconnect with my family.

The more we talked, the more I realized that my daughter having Down syndrome was not a "life of hopelessness" for her or my family. Sure, things would be different and few people would understand those differences, but it would still be a great life. My daughter would not be some monster who could not accomplish anything in life. My daughter would be a unique person who would have her own interests, hobbies, and dreams. Supporting her and teaching her, like any other child, would help her accomplish great things in life and to become the person she was called to be. She would only be limited in life if Jana and I tried to limit her by sheltering her from the realities of the world.

These families with Down syndrome children understood the pain I was feeling and never tried to belittle or fix my problems. Instead they listened first and then offered their own experiences second. They gave me support during a time when support from my own community was incomplete because no one at our school had a child with Down syndrome. These parents could relate to me and understand the disappointment I felt. Talking to these families for over a year offered me the chance to heal through sharing. Facing this crisis alone would have led to death or abandonment, but when these families came alongside me during my darkest hour, they refused to let me give up. Instead they offered me a realistic future of pain and joy in raising a daughter with Down syndrome.

The first moment of healing occurred when Marley was several months old. We were getting ready for church and I went to get her out of her crib. As I reached down to get her, I saw a little smile come across her face. I was so excited that I began crying and yelled for Jana to come in the room. It seems extremely silly now, but that smile gave me the push I needed to try and connect with my daughter. It was the first time I saw her as Marley ,and not my baby with Down syndrome.

The relationship I have built these past few years with Marley has been amazing. She is truly the joy of my life. Of course, I still worry about her future. I am not sure what kind of father would not worry about their child's future, but I am learning to trust God with that struggle. She is behind on some milestones for her age, but she also does some things that other children her age do not do. People in our community love her and I am amazed at how she is already changing lives.

I still wish she did not have Down syndrome, but I have accepted that this is her life. Everyone is different and most people would love to change things about themselves, but that is not the basis of our lives. The reality is we are given the life we need to better this world and we need to embrace those differences. My daughter has opened my eyes to a world beyond myself. The day the doctor told us Marley had Down syndrome, I hated everything and everyone associated with this genetic disorder. Today I can proudly say that Down syndrome has changed my life for the better. Down syndrome is not something that we simply tolerate in our society; but rather it is something that can teach us to be better people in this world. Everyone, regardless of their similarities or differences, has the potential to mold our lives for the better.

My family and I are not looking for handouts or exceptions. We know that we will forever be changed and that our daughter will forever be different. But you know what? That is ok. When people look at Marley now and make the sympathetic face that suggests, "I'm sorry your daughter has Down syndrome," I think if only they knew the beauty of Marley's life. Instead of running from the Down syndrome delusion, we have embraced it with open arms and accepted the wonder of raising a child with Down syndrome. There will always be difficult days—and that comes with the territory with raising any child—but when those special moments come in Marley's life, we take the time to "smell the roses" and cherish them as a family.

One night while eating dinner with friends, a couple commented about how our family had changed during this experience. Our friends encouraged us to do something to share our story with the world. I thought about this for several months, and one night while reading, I thought about the fear that had crippled me upon hearing that Marley was diagnosed with Down syndrome. This prompted me to look at ways I could encourage other fathers in that desperate time of confusion.

When Marley was born, the only thing I could think about was fear—fear of her future, fear of the world mistreating her, fear of her health, fear of my family's reaction, fear of everything associated with Marley and Down syndrome. What I quickly realized that night at dinner was that I no longer carried many of those fears and burdens in my life. The main thing that had helped me overcome those fears was the reality of Marley. Meeting her and spending time with her made me realize that she was very much like any other child. The fears that I wrote about in the previous chapter are now associated with her future health and wellness. The little girl I had rocked to sleep was nothing like the vision I had of Down syndrome when the doctor first told us about it.

One night after putting Marley to bed, I started writing out a conversation between a mother and her unborn child. This video helped launch our website and an awareness campaign we started called "If They Had a Voice" (www.iftheyhadavoice.org). I thought this would be an excellent way to help parents alleviate the fears they might have while pregnant. It was difficult for me to build a relationship with Marley at first, and I quickly realized that it would have been even more difficult if I could not even see Marley. But the video focuses on what a child with Down syndrome "can" be versus what we are told they "cannot" be by our society. Here is the introduction from our campaign:

> *Right now, a mother has been asked to make a choice. She must decide to either keep or abort a child who is different from her original plan. This baby will always be different and there is nothing she can do to change that fact. Will she choose to take a different path, or listen to society that says a Down syndrome child is already broken at birth? The hardest day of her life has suddenly been filled with people telling her that aborting this child would be best for her family.*
>
> *I had believed this lie for an entire year. An entire year of fatherhood was taken from me because I could only see my daughter as a disabled child that I created. The happy*

moments that I should have been enjoying the first year were masked by a deep depression that included thoughts of divorce and suicide. For thirty plus years, I had believed a lie that special needs children were nothing more than a burden on their families and society, but my wife and daughter did not give up on me. My one-year-old daughter refused to stop loving me. She appeared to be like every other child, but that voice kept telling me she was different. Finally, after months of battling depression, something happened that spoke to my soul. My daughter gave me a kiss without any warning. At that moment, I knew my daughter needed a father and not another doubter. Every mother must make a choice and I respect that difficult process, but I want every expectant mother to hear both sides of the story. Raising any child is difficult, but it makes me sick to think what beautiful moments I would have missed these past two years if I had taken a different path than staying with my daughter.

The **If They Had a Voice** campaign is our effort to encourage other families. The families I connected with during my dark times were always there to help me during this journey. We want to do the same now, and this is the reason for the campaign. We encourage you to join us and share this with your community. This is not a fundraiser and requires very little from you. Our only goal is for families to consider the future they might have if they raise a child with Down syndrome. We are not here to judge or condemn mothers and the choices they must make. We don't have the time or the resources to focus on changing laws or mass opinions. Our only hope is that every mother who is given a diagnosis of Down syndrome for her unborn child considers the great things that her child can bring to this world. Every situation is different and every family has to make their own choice. We believe, however, that the positive light and rewards we have experienced in raising Marley should be shared before a mother suddenly makes a difficult choice. Giving an expectant mother both sides of the argument in raising a child with Down syndrome should be a priority for us as a caring society. We are not here to paint the disability with only rainbows, but we fully understand the beauty that can come from a charming daughter who just happens to have Down syndrome. Our life was fairly plain and mundane—like most families—until Marley arrived. Now this journey has ushered in a new understanding of love, acceptance, and compassion that we would have missed out on our entire lives without our precious chromosomal gifted daughter, Marley.

Do Something as a Family

Find a cause you care about and support it. My cause was forced on me when Marley was born. Before her birth, I knew nothing about Down syndrome or special needs. Now it has become a constant fixture in my daily life. The decision was a little easier for me because it affected my immediate family. Maybe you have a similar situation in your family. There are so many problems in this world and few people fighting the good fight against them. Find that one cause that excites your family and get behind it. Make it a tradition to be involved with that cause or organization. It will not only benefit your family, but it will also assist those who need help. We need to learn to put others first as there is no greater lesson that can be taught to our children. Make "caring for others" part of your family tradition by giving the time needed to help a cause that is important to you and your family.

A Note to Marley

Love is patient, love is kind. It does not envy, it does not boast, it is not proud. It does not dishonor others, it is not self-seeking, it is not easily angered, it keeps no record of wrongs. Love does not delight in evil but rejoices with the truth.
(1 Corinthians 13:4-6 NIV)

Marley, today I came home from work, and I heard you yelling when I pulled up on my scooter. From the street I could hear your innocent voice calling out to me—"Da-ddy, Da-ddy." As I walked up the steps towards our sliding glass front door, I saw you standing there with your arms up in the air waiting for a hug. Only God knows how long you would stand there waiting for me so you could give me your welcome home hug.

As I bend down and hug your little toddler body, I can barely hold back the tears of shame that I now carry in my daily life, the shame I have of abandoning you mentally and emotionally for the first year of your life. How I long to go back then and know what I know today as I hug you so tight that you begin to giggle. You have shaped my life for the better and taught me about a love

I could never truly understand before your birth.

When I wrote the CNN article, I read comments about the hatred you would feel towards me one day. How could I share the darkest thoughts of my soul about my own daughter? Many parents were sure to point out that one day you would not only hate me, but refuse to love me because of how I treated you during your first year. As I finish this book, I accept that you may abandon me the same way I abandoned you that first year. If that fate comes, I will fully accept it, because that would only be a fair response to my failures as a father to you. The day is coming that you will not see me as the hero hugging you now, but before that day comes, I want you to understand that I believe true healing comes through honesty.

This book is because of you, and the change in my life would never have occurred without you. Today, I have a love for you that I could have never imagined or comprehended before the words *Down syndrome* entered our family's life. In the next few moments, I am going to share with you some struggles I have encountered and things that you will have to face in this world. My love for you and the journey of our lives need to be shared because many fathers out there are receiving news that will forever change them,

You are a beautiful blessing who has taught me many things these first few years. It started out difficult for me, but I promise you I will be right here loving and caring for you until we meet our father in heaven. When you were born, I was scared. Even before I knew about your extra chromosome, I was scared. The idea of having another person in my life to care for worried me day and night. I never really told Mommy, but I was fearful of being a terrible father. From the moment you were born, I was anxious about you and your health. The only things I could think about were the problems that you might have instead of enjoying the beautiful person you are.

When the doctor told me that you had Down syndrome, I went into panic mode. I knew you were different. The problem was that I could not see past the diagnosis. You are different, just like how I am different, and how Mommy is different. You are the most beautiful person I have ever met and the sweetest girl in the world, except when you don't nap (just kidding!). Now I look forward to spending time with you every day. Things I used to love to do like play basketball, watch ESPN, and listen to the Orioles all come second after you. You have made me a better husband, father, and person in this world. The bear hugs we share are some of the happiest moments of my life. Our secret kisses through the mosquito net on your crib are the final nightcap I cherish every evening before going to bed. The little things like chowing down on hamburgers together because momma refuses to eat that junk food would have been nonexistent without you. I pray to God that we are able to spend many years together, and I thank him for the great blessing that you are in my life.

I am sorry for letting fear blind me when you were first born. Unfortunately, some people in this world think like I did. They will only see you as someone different and may not want to talk to you. Marley, I am sorry, and I pray that it rarely happens in your life. The world can be a difficult and confusing place. People like me don't always understand things that are different, so we run from them. I know that is not fair. You have opened my eyes to a new world of acceptance and understanding of people regardless of their differences.

I pray that you will forgive me for my ignorance during the first year of your life. Looking back now, I am so ashamed of the way I ignored you and the pain I caused you and Mommy. Now, three years since your birth, I see the perfect little daughter whom I could have never imagined. You are more than I had ever hoped for before you were born. Your determination is amazing, and I know you are going to accomplish great things in this world. You have changed our families, our community, and the city of Bangkok. Everyone knows who Marley is because you carry a heart of acceptance and love.

As I close, I pray that you will one day forgive me for my insecurities and doubts. I am going to spend the remainder of my life teaching you, loving you, helping you, and protecting you. You are a gem in this world that some people may never choose to experience. I know there will be days that we will cry together, but there will be more days that we laugh and dance together.

The world can be a cruel place but the great news is that you will overcome it. You have a bloodline of fighters, and I already see the fight you will bring against anyone who doubts you! God is on your side, and he has a greater plan for you than he ever had for Mommy and me. The things he has done with your life these first three years are amazing. I love you, my beautiful daughter, and thank you for entering my life so I could see the beauty that only you could show me. —"Da-ddy"

Epilogue

Then you will know the truth, and the truth will set you free. (John 8:32 NIV)

I chose the phrase "Failing at Fatherhood" because it best describes the view I have of myself these past first three years as a Dad. I have made many mistakes and most of these actions, I am ashamed of. The day will come when I will have to sit down and explain all of this to my lovely daughter, and I dread it more than anything else.

Many people have asked me, "Why share this when it will be out in the world for others to criticize?" I have wrestled with this dilemma for a long time because I knew that this wasn't a moneymaking project for my family. Most likely, only a little revenue will come my way from this book, but I am sure a lot of feedback will be headed to my inbox. It came down to what I believed in as a Christian. If I am going to stand up and say that I believe in God, then I have to believe in God's word, the Bible. There is a story in the Bible that I referred to back when I was contemplating publishing the CNN article and writing this book. Here is a piece of it from the scriptures.

Genesis 22:1-12 (New International Version):

> *Some time later God tested Abraham. He said to him, "Abraham!" "Here I am," he replied. Then God said, "Take your son, your only son, whom you love—Isaac—and go to the region of Moriah. Sacrifice him there as a burnt offering on a mountain I will show you." Early the next morning Abraham got up and loaded his donkey. He took with him two of his servants and his son Isaac. When he had cut enough wood for the burnt offering, he set out for the place God had told him about.*
>
> *On the third day Abraham looked up and saw the place in the distance. He said to his servants, "Stay here with the donkey while I and the boy go over there. We will worship and then we will come back to you." Abraham took the wood for the burnt offering and placed it on his son Isaac, and he himself carried the fire and the knife. As the two of them went on together, Isaac spoke up and said to his father Abraham, "Father?" "Yes, my son?" Abraham replied. "The fire and wood are here," Isaac said, "but where is the lamb for the burnt offering?" Abraham answered, "God himself will provide the lamb for the burnt offering, my son." And the two of them went on together.*
>
> *When they reached the place God had told him about, Abraham built an altar there and arranged the wood on it. He bound his son Isaac and laid him on the altar, on top of the wood. Then he reached out his hand and took the knife to slay his son. But the angel of the* LORD *called out to him from heaven, "Abraham! Abraham!" "Here I am," he replied. "Do not lay a hand on the boy," he said. "Do not do anything to him. Now I know that you fear God, because you have not withheld from me your son, your only son."*

This is one of those stories that Bible critics love to attack. How could a loving God ask someone to sacrifice his or her own son? What a terrible example of a "loving" God in scriptures. I must admit that this passage has always perplexed me until recently. The idea of murdering our own child for a being that many of us have not even seen—what is the point of believing in a God like that? For me, it came down to the belief that my daughter was not the most important person or thing in my life. Let me say that again: *my daughter is not the most important thing in life*. That is hard to say and even harder to believe, but let me tell you why I now believe I understand this story about Abraham a little bit better.

The most important thing in life is not our children, but *helping* our children accomplish the calling God has for them. By sharing this story, I am in theory surrendering my daughter and opening the door to my initial thoughts regarding Down syndrome. It was never that I hated my daughter; it was the fact that I hated her having Down syndrome. If I did not share my story, then everything Marley has taught me would be lost once my life was over. What if a mother decides to keep her unborn child because she hears about Marley's story? What if a father decides to come home one night instead of leaving his family for a life of freedom? And finally, what if someone takes a step out of the pit of darkness instead of ending everything in death? People need guidance and hope, and this is not my story, but the story of Marley transforming my purpose, belief, approach, and ultimately, me. What a miracle that would be if my daughter that has been labeled as "broken," actually helped saved lives, families, and other children!

Abraham did not want to kill his only son, but he knew that if God was asking him to do it, then there was a greater purpose. The same is true with our lives. That is why this question I keep prodding you with—*is there a God?*—is so critical for you. Your entire direction in life is guided by a belief or lack of a belief in a Creator.

I don't want Marley to walk in one day and say, "Daddy, why did you not want me when I was born?" I know that day is coming and I will endure that crisis when it darkens my door. But facing that day is so much better than the alternative of not being honest with God, my daughter, or myself, and letting this story go untold. New fathers and mothers are hurting, and they need to know that there are other parents in this world that can help show them a glimpse of the joy they will have with their new son or daughter.

The point of this book is not to make a few dollars at my daughter or wife's expense, but instead help others understand that fatherhood can be extremely difficult. The silver lining here is that with help, we can navigate through it. No father should ever look down at his child and think, "I don't want this child." No child should ever grow up in this harsh world without a father there to support him or her in every step of the way.

It was not Marley's birth that led me to fail as a father, but it was the previous issues that were never resolved which led to inadequate healing. If sharing my deepest thoughts helps someone start a relationship with God, convinces a father to stay with his children, or helps parents mend their relationships with their own children, then I believe it is worth every bit of criticism. Marley knows I love her, and when that day of reckoning comes for our family, I can only trust that God and Marley will both forgive me for my past transgressions.

Thank you for reading ***Failing at Fatherhood*** by Jack Barr. For more information about Jack and his story, please visit: www.iftheyhadavoice.org

Also, we invite you to visit our website: www.trinitygracepress.com

CPSIA information can be obtained
at www.ICGtesting.com
Printed in the USA
FFOW01n0852151014
8061FF